Gorilla Warfare Against The Bureaucratic State

Confessions of a Lefty Libertarian

by Michael Silverstein

Silverwood Publishing, Philadelphia

Illustrated and designed by Kay Wood
Printed in the United States of America
First edition April 2015

Other books by Michael Silverstein:

The Devil's Dictionary Of Wall Street

Fifteen Feet Beneath Manhattan

The Bellman's Revenge

Murder At Bernstein's

*A Dyspeptic's Guide To Contemporary
American Politics (In Verse)*

*The Chronicles Of Selig Cartwright,
Goldman Sachs Washroom Attendant*

For more information about purchasing any of
these books direct from the author
and autographed copies contact:
mike@wallstreetpoet.com

Table Of Contents

*This book's definition of "gorilla" — An individual who takes
on hopeless but worthwhile causes; who disrupts (at least for
awhile) the machinations of deeply entrenched interests; or who
causes a change (at least to some extent) in ossified thinking;
and who does these things while wearing gorilla slippers.*

I.
A Star Named Sol
(Enter The Gorilla)

In early 1974 I was vouchsafed a vision in Miami Beach.

At the time I was writing for a music magazine. It had a deal
with a Miami hotel called The Beau Ravage. The hotel got ad
space in the magazine. Employees of the publication, whether
on assignment or vacation, got free rooms in the hotel. I took the
opportunity of an assignment in Miami to enjoy a cheap vacation
with my wife Suzanne and our young son Jonathan.

One morning, en famille, we were descending in the hotel's
elevator. It was a slow-moving contraption that took a long
time between floors. At the stop down from our own the doors
opened and a woman got on. The doors closed again and we all
descended, slowly, very slowly, the woman staring at us very
hard all the while.

She was a strange apparition. Strange, at least, to someone who
did not live in the Sunbelt.

Her skin had the consistency of exterior wall paint on a very old
house just before the owner decides to install aluminum siding.
Her face was a collage of penciled lines on peeling plains. Her
nails looked like they were manicured in a dish of piranhas. She
had a breast line compounded of expired modeling aspirations

and first generation silicon surgery. Her summer dress was a
polka dot affair more revealing than wise. The handbag she
carried was shaped like a valentine, and big enough to hold the
spare tire of a Volvo.

For reasons that defy rational explanation, I was absolutely and
immediately certain that our new companion had been stalking
us. My wife Suzanne clearly felt the same way. Unconsciously,
like musk oxen, we pressed closer together to shield young Jon,
then all three of us looked up and watched the numbers on the
elevator's floor indicator sink at a sickening crawl.

When we reached ground level, before we could disembark into
the lobby, the woman spoke.

"Ever think of living in Ft. Pierce?"

"Well, no," I confided, moving to brush by her and into the
lobby that was now visible through the open elevator door. She
had the way blocked, however, and was not about to let us exit
until our business was completed. I faltered. Like the wedding
guest in thrall to an ancient mariner, I was riveted to the spot,
destined to stare into her dead eyes and hear her tale, like it or
no.

"You people can help me," she continued. "And I can help you.
It's that simple."

"It does sound easy," Suzanne chimed in. Our marriage was not
going well by this time and she had apparently decided that if a
blood sacrifice were needed to extricate Jon, a mother was more
important to his future upbringing than a dad. "You two can talk
it over while the boy and I get some breakfast."

Again, the woman who barred our way refused to move aside.
Suzanne, too, fell back to her place in the elevator. Beaten.

"You get breakfast as part of the package. Free." Her eyes were cold as pewter. Her voice an even duller shade of flat.

"Ft. Pierce? Breakfast? Free?" I repeated, trying not to excite her.

"Right."

She reached into her bag. Took out some kind of invitations. Shoved them in my direction. There was no shake in the fingers holding those bits of paper. None. They say you get that way once the actual death throes are over.

"Take."

I took.

"Here's the deal. You go next door. The hotel right up the sidewalk, on the left as you walk out the front entrance. On the ground floor is a meeting room. You hear their pitch for property in Ft. Piece, which is on the other side of Florida, by the way. They give you a bus ride over in case you want to see the place before you buy it. But as far as my own commission is concerned, it doesn't matter whether you buy property or not."

"You get your commission either way," I said in order to make sure I had it down correctly.

"Either way." She nodded.

"Right." I affirmed.

"And just for going you get free tickets for a boat ride around the Keys. When it's over, we'll meet back here. I get the commission, maybe I'll buy a gift for the little boy. What's his name?"

"Timmy," replied my wife quickly. I smiled agreeably. My wife was sharp. Without Jon's correct first name, without his fingernail clippings or tufts of his hair, our captor couldn't do anything really bad to him. Provided, of course, we cooperated.

"Until later," said the apparition with finality. She closed her bag with a snap and walked out of the elevator. She did not look left or right before disappearing around a bend in the hall.

"I'm hungry," said Jon.

So we went next door for breakfast, and to hear about buying property in Ft. Pierce.

The property pitch took place in a room big enough to hold an Ethel Merman concert. It was presided over by a half-dozen presenters wearing Oleg Cassini sport jackets in colors that spanned the spectrum from lemon to lime.

One of them lounged at a speaker's lectern darting looks down at his watch and up at his audience, clearly weighing the merits of waiting for another fish or two to arrive versus the possibility that some of the dozen or so mini-schools (couples and a few children) already there would slip away. Another two sat on either side of this speaker-to-be, legs crossed, feigning interest and sincerity. Badly. The remaining three were strategically stationed near the exits as greeters, and if necessary, detainers.

All of the guests in attendance looked vaguely lost. The politely overlooked reality of Miami Beach then and now, and indeed, virtually all resorts anywhere in the world since the dawn of time, is that these places are dull as dirt. Once you have taken the waters, or dipped in the ocean, or hurtled down the slopes a couple of times, once you have sampled the pricey, undistinguished fare they put on plates as substitutes for cuisine, there is nothing much to do except try, desperately, to encounter an experience that will allow you to tell those back home something that makes your recent waste of time and money seem worth the effort.

Our fellow prospective Ft. Pierce property buyers were a totally random group of East Coast and Middle Americans dressed in unattractive swimsuits and floppy hats who determinedly attacked the bagels, doughnuts, coffee and juice set before us in lieu of having to confess to others in the group the embarrassing ennui that had attracted them here. Aware that our own participation was the product of pure fear rather than boredom, we naturally enjoyed a feeling of superiority.

The meeting was called to order at last. The pitch was made. It included the usual slide show, the passing out of brochures, several family style jokes based on coy allusions to bathrooms, and a rather heroic attempt to link the family values that pervaded crime-free Ft. Pierce with the certainty of increasing property values in the planned community in which these gentlemen were selling interests.

Thus prepped, and presumably also filled with gratitude for the meal that had been set before us at no cost, the sales team fell among us. One couple or family grouping per team member.

The guy we drew came over and shook my hand, beaming at the little lady and our charming offspring all the while. He was a very large man with ham-hock hands and a mane of exceptionally well-tended white hair. I put him down for retired military, vintage NCO or warrant officer, old Panama Canal Zone maybe, currently short on cash, slowly going to seed in another adopted tropics.

"I think I understand why you came here," he said, looking at me hard and deep the way guys do when the subject has gone serious. "I'm Italian. I understand how important it is to find the right place to raise a family."

Suzanne nodded with exaggerated gravity. She did it less to make fun of our host than to make it clear to me that a head of a household who allowed his loved ones to endure this kind of crap was a nincompoop. Jon meanwhile, was looking down at a half-eaten doughnut, wondering whether the colored stuff on it was some variant of powdered sugar or mold.

Then Tom (that was his name) explained the property offering in more detail. His company would send us on a five-hour bus ride to their new development on the west side of Florida. The trip and the arrangements that went with it would not cost us a nickel. Absolutely free. In return, we were merely expected to give him a $1,500 check (or credit card voucher) as a sign of our own good faith, a sum that would be promptly returned if we did not like what we saw, or applied to the down payment if we did.

"No," I said.

He feigned surprise at my instant response. "But..."

I had actually eaten two of the doughnuts from the stack that Jon's own careful examination had caused him to spurn after a couple of bites. My stomach felt like I had dined on buckshot. Even a nincompoop has his limits. "No!"

Tom just shrugged. Another brace of pigeons was waiting at the next table. He reached into his pocket and placed three tickets on our table. "For the cruise of the Keys. You'll like it." He winked. "Honest."

Which was how we got to take a cruise around the Florida Keys. Which is how I got my introduction to the great star Sol. Which is how the latent, sleeping gorilla inside me came to be activated.

The day of my fateful cruise in the Florida Keys was exquisite. Clear as glass with a light rippling wind that gave our little tour boat a delightfully pleasant bounce. Our tour guide told us how the tiny islands, the Keys, had come into being. How they were developed and became places where rich people built their pleasure palaces. He took special note of one of the more elaborate of these structures.

"You see that building that looks a bit like a chimney, the one next to the main house?" he shouted over the wind through his little dunce cap-shaped tour guide megaphone. "That's a solar water heater. It was built in 1928. The people on this key didn't like oil heat. They made their money in coal, you know."

We chuckled on cue.

"Nineteen twenty-eight," he repeated.

And again. "Nineteen twenty-eight."

It was now early 1974. Only one thing was uppermost on the minds of most Americans—the Arab Oil Embargo that had been declared a few months earlier.

This was the latest in a nasty run of national stumbles. We had just lost our first-ever war in Vietnam. We had our first-ever unelected president, Gerald Ford, because the duly elected president and vice-president, Richard Nixon and Spiro Agnew, had been forced from office by scandals. Then, all of a sudden, on top of everything else, someone hit the brakes in the petroleum market, sent gasoline and heating oil prices through the roof, and our whole way of life seemed threatened.

What was to be done about energy? That was the question all the pundits were asking. Seize the Middle Eastern oil fields by force? Adjust to a more simple, less energy-intensive economy? Rapidly develop energy resources that were not subject to embargo? And if the later option were pursued, what resources should they be? Natural gas? Coal? Hydro? Nuclear? Wood? Wind? What?

And here I was. In 1974. In the opening days of this energy crisis. Being told about a solar water heater that had been operating successfully since 1928!

In a flash I saw it all. Saw it whole. Saw it complete. The entire enchilada from griddle to sour cream and garnish. Solar energy would save America. My destiny was to make it happen. I had seen the vision, and its name was Sol.

Later that afternoon, back at our hotel, walking toward the elevator in the lobby, we again encountered the apparition with scaling skin and dead eyes. She seemed inclined to pass us by without a word, but thought better of it as we were about to gratefully reciprocate.

"I got my commission."

"Oh good," Suzanne replied irritably, pushing at the elevator button.

"I'll bet you liked the boat ride," the apparition added in my direction. Then smiled in a way that made me think of chemotherapy. "I'll get that toy for your little one. What's his name?"

"Chester," Suzanne shot back over her shoulder, banging the elevator button with a fist.

"Nice little boy," was the last thing the instrument of my enlightenment said before disappearing down the hall and out of our lives.

Crisis creates opportunities. It opens new vistas for new people. It's a time when credentials matter less than smarts, when almost anyone with a clear idea about where to go or what to do can get a hearing. Crisis is also when new ideas, or in some cases, very old ideas, can emerge or reemerge and receive serious consideration.

The fact that my just awakened determination to solarize America was not in any way supported by a technical background, academic standing, or specialized business acumen did not, therefore, strike me as terribly significant. In early 1974 no one was especially prominent in the solar field. Indeed, there was no functioning "field" worth mentioning before the oil embargo came along.

My first task was therefore to learn a few basics about solar that I could use to impress people even more ignorant on the subject than myself. I found this quick study inspiring. Here's a few things I collected along the way.

People have always helped regulate temperatures in their homes by using different colored paints or special materials to absorb or reflect solar radiations. By the eighteenth century, when clear glass started being produced cheaply and in quantity, it even became possible to construct many thousand totally solar-heated structures. Greenhouses. So while efficient, predictable, and cost effective solar space heating was still a fairly tricky affair for human habitations in the oil embargoed 1970's, the technology of such heating was neither unknown nor exotic.

The same was even more true when it came to solar water heating. The Romans used the sun to heat water for their bathhouses. Solar water heaters were operational in parts of the American South by the early 1800's. They had become a commercial commonplace in Arizona and New Mexico (and the Florida Keys) by the 1920s, before natural gas became available in sufficient qualities and co-opted the water heating markets there. Still, by the early 1970's, there were literally millions of functioning solar water heaters around the world in countries such as Australia, Israel and Japan.

While decades would pass before solar electric technologies would come on line in a significant way, solar heating technologies were simple and well understood. Unlike nuclear energy, there was no issue of health or safety to warrant direct government intervention in the marketplace to protect consumers. A basic solar water heater is really just a water filled metal canister painted black with a hose on the bottom. The black paint absorbs solar energy, heats the water in the canister, which then flows downthrough the hose. A boy scout project.

True, there was an unfavorable price differential in the 1970's between the cost of solar water heating systems and other energy systems in most parts of this country, even where costs of competing fossil fuels were rising rapidly. So completely had solar captured the national imagination in these years, however, that by itself this price differential would not have been a major impediment to large-scale acceptance.

After all, natural gas, when it first entered the energy mass market in the 1920's, was much more expensive than coal, the then dominant fuel for home heating purposes. It was nonetheless readily accepted by Americans anxious to use what was then billed as "the ultimate clean fuel," and the replacement for "ashes on Saturday," the weekly need to collect and dispose of coal ash in the basement.

Though development and marketability of solar cells (to generate electricity) would require more time to come on line, solar heating products and systems (especially water heating products and systems) would certainly have made rapid inroads into the American home and buildings markets with very modest government help backed by a powerful dose of the bully pulpit. Unfortunately, the politics of the day intervened.

The star Sol became a captive of consumer activists and Washington planner bureaucrats. I was forced to witness the trashing of a personal vision I held dear.

There's an old salesman trick. You trawl your products. You bring them out one by one and float them past a prospective customer, waiting for a nod or a little chuckle of appreciation. Then you pretend that all the other goods in your line never existed and proceed to sell like crazy what your customer already seems prepared to buy.

I've experienced a similar phenomenon as a writer. A lot of ideas are floated. Few are acknowledged much less applauded. With solar energy, though, my reception was immediate and fulsome.

I remember coming back to my then hometown of Boston from Miami with a vague idea of solarizing America. It was nothing specific, it had yet to take a form, and it was certainly not on top of my mind when I called the editor of The New England Business Journal shortly after my return from Miami in hopes of selling a freelance idea to supplement my music magazine salary.

"Hey Murray. Got a minute?"

He responded with his usual guttural and surly affirmative. Murray Garfunkel had one of those great newspaperman's voices that sound like it came from under an eyeshade. Without ever meeting the man you knew he smoked unfiltered Camels and used a noisy old typewriter with no cover hiding the key supports.

"Thirty seconds," grunted Murray.

"I got something good while I was down in Miami."

"See a doctor about it. I'm busy."

"Murray, listen. There are some really interesting business tie-ins between music companies down there and the music chains in Boston."

"If they're so interesting, why am I not interested?"

"You're a hard man. A vacation guide story, Murray. How about a vacation guide? Everybody in Boston goes to Florida in the winter. You could get ads from travel bureaus. The visitor bureau in Miami."

"Seventeen...sixteen...fifteen..." he counted ominously.

"Solar energy."

The counting stopped. I could almost hear the hook catch in Murray's pulpy upper lip.

"So, I'm listening."

That was how I came to write my first solar energy story in early 1974. In the New England Business Journal. For all I know it may well have been the first story about solar energy as a potential growth industry, a big-ticket business, done anywhere in the United States in the wake of the Arab Oil Embargo. Certainly, it generated an extraordinary response in the local academic and consulting communities of New England.

At first glance this may sound odd. New England, after all, together with its economic and political capital Boston, is not exactly the sunshine capital of America. You might expect that while solar energy would capture the imagination of Californians and Floridians, it would be of little interest in these northeastern latitudes.

This notion, I quickly realized, was wrong because of local economics prevailing at this time. The market value of a new energy contender like solar is related to the cost of the energy it replaces. The New England area was then at the end of a very long energy supply chain and had to import more than eighty-five percent of its fossil fuels, most in the form of home heating oil produced by OPEC charter member Venezuela.

Thus, while Boston might get just seventy percent of the radiant sunshine of Yuma, Arizona, residents of this latter city were still paying only half as much for their natural gas heating even after hydrocarbon prices began to soar in 1974. And Yumerians (or are they Yumites?), unlike Bostonians, did not have nearly as great a need for heating in the winter.

This largely explains why my own work to solarize the country was mostly directed at a New England audience. At least initially. My entrance into the New England energy quagmire of this period also coincided with the appearance of the first "Freeze A Yankee, Cut Off His Oil Supply" bumper stickers on cars south of the Mason-Dixon Line. My soon to gain great popularity response to this sentiment in Boston was: "Screw Texas. Go solar!"

Things happened fast after that first New England Business Journal article. Soon I was doing "solar-is-here" pieces for all sorts of local publications. This quickly led to print appearances in national trade publications, business magazines, and general interest dailies and monthlies. In all, I was to write scores of articles and a couple of books about solar over the next half decade.

One immediate upshot of the New England Business Journal story involved researchers at the Arthur D. Little consulting firm in Cambridge, Massachusetts who I had interviewed for one of my pieces. They put me in touch with a group of techies at the Massachusetts Institute of Technology who had just formed The New England Solar Energy Association. Within weeks, while still then basically a music magazine writer, I was on that group's board of directors.

Passing the hat at a solar association meeting I raised enough money to place the region's first newspaper ad heralding the coming of a New England-based solar industry. A friend had an answering machine (something of a rarity in those days) and we used it to set up the area's first solar hotline. You called in, heard a recording of me describing solar energy's wonderful future, and if you left your name and address on the tape were rewarded with a collection of my recent writings on the subject. Free and mailed at my own expense.

And then there was Solar Citizens of Massachusetts, the lobbying group that consumed much of my non-writing activity in 1974 and 1975. A group that consisted of me and a letterhead.

Conning the media has always been one of America's great non-athletic sporting activities. Solar Citizens marked my own first full-blown participation in this blood, sweat, and shit-soaked arena.

Since the press no longer cares about what individuals think, and since serious media time and space is only allocated to certified spokespeople for well-funded and/or mass membership organizations, it has become necessary for singular persons with innovative ideas like myself to pretend to be mere vocal instruments of such organizational collectives. Hence, Solar Citizens of Massachusetts.

This history of this boutique lobby holds a rather poignant place in the national political history of solar energy. For better or worse, I, in the guise of Solar Citizens, played a major role in putting solar energy near the top of the post-election agenda of the 39th President of these United States, James Earl Carter, Jr.

It came about this way:

Massachusetts' presidential primaries before 1976 (or since for that matter) were rarely important in choosing the eventual two party candidates for the Oval Office. Presidential aspirants usually sank enormous time and energy trying to look good in the nation's first primary in New Hampshire. They then focused their efforts on fund-raising activities during the next few weeks in preparation for big state primaries in New York and California, followed by the "super" regional primary in several southern states.

In 1976, however, an early Massachusetts primary would play a surprisingly important role in choosing the winning candidates.

This became clear to me eight months before the Massachusetts showdown, in the summer of 1975. It also became clear to me that if one could appear to head a large and well-organized alternative energy association with firm policy views, at a time when energy policy was the big national issue, in an early primary state when an unusually large number of contending candidates were all vying for attention, none yet with a clear front runner, any large and well-organized appearing group could reap a critical (if short-lived) political significance. And from this perspective, this group would be in a position to get the next President of the United States, whoever that turned out to be, to take serious notice of solar energy.

So in June of 1975 I started writing the presidential campaign committees of all then declared candidates, adding new committees to my list as they were announced. Responses to these first contacts were nil. Initially, no one seemed to care about Solar Citizens of Massachusetts or its demands for a "candidate statement on solar." I nonetheless felt certain that my correspondence was not just being thrown away, but was being saved for possible future follow up.

This hunch proved sound. By December of 1975, as the bulging field of now-declared candidates approached the primary starting line, with Massachusetts near the front of that line, I began getting regular calls from election committees asking what, exactly, my group wanted. I replied that what we wanted were position papers, as explicit as possible, about how solar would fit into the energy policies of a new administration.

My aim at the time was not to make the solar energy policy of a new administration. It was merely to get the candidates for president to have such a policy.

It worked.

By the time Massachusetts' primary day rolled around, every

one of the fourteen Democratic and Republican candidates, except Governors George Wallace and Ronald Reagan, had provided Solar Citizens with a solar energy position paper. It was the very first time any of these worthies had made an official pronouncement on the subject.

Aptness of thought was naturally not much in evidence in most of these efforts. President Ford's position paper was just a page of rambling platitudes. The one from soon-to-be-elected Jimmy Carter, on the other hand, was a tightly spaced affair filled with the sort of technical enthusiasm one encounters with people who once served on nuclear submarines. The solar position of Governor Milton Shapp of Pennsylvania, America's first serious (oh all right, semi-serious) Jewish candidate for the Oval Office, appeared to have been slapped together during a coffee klatch of Philadelphia product liability attorneys.

This was nonetheless fine with me. Content here was less important than awareness. My problem came when it was actually time to gather up what I had caused to be created.

Since my intention was merely to elicit fresh thinking rather than disseminate the results of this thinking, the days just before the primary in Massachusetts were something of an embarrassment. When the campaign office of each candidate called to say their position papers were ready for pick up and distribution, I was obliged to drive by each campaign office, proclaim myself to be a volunteer working with Solar Citizens, pick up their offerings, and drive away. Once around the corner I would break into a carton, take out a few dozen position papers for my personal files, and deposit the rest in a nearby dumpster.

This procedure caused me few qualms until I went to pick up the solar energy position papers of Fred Harris, a Senator from Oklahoma, whose chief campaign assets were a liberal populism and a charming Indian wife named LaDonna. Every other candidate had provided Solar Citizens (that is to say me) with a few thousand flyers, enough to fill three or four boxes. Harris headquarters had produced enough solar literature to fill twenty cartons, done on costly recycled paper, all bearing a prominent union "bug" that alerted the cognoscenti to the fact that the printing job had cost three times more than a non-union printer would have charged.

I was assisted loading this political tonnage into my car by a young and very garrulous Harris campaign worker. As I was about to drive off he confided:

"You know, Fred and LaDonna really believe in solar. It's almost like a religion with them. They genuinely appreciate you folks helping us get the word out. You have a statewide network, I hope."

"Statewide? Well..." I hesitated. "Sure. In the sense that our membership is spread evenly across the state. Absolutely."

He patted me on the shoulder. "Fred and LaDonna also send their personal assurances that if Fred does get elected, he will positively put a solar water heater on the White House as his first official act."

I left this kid quite certain that the Harris effort to win the favor of Solar Citizens was near the top of their Massachusetts campaign planning and a major element in a hoped-for primary upset—a hope that found its way into a dumpster in Cambridge, Massachusetts a few moments later.

Fred. LaDonna. I'm sorry. It was nothing personal. Honest.

As a consolation prize (admittedly a very modest one), I sent a copy of the Harris solar position paper, which included the promise to put a solar water heater on the White House, to the issues director of the Carter campaign right after Carter's victory in Massachusetts. A "please look this over carefully" note on the

Solar Citizens letterhead signed by its executive director went with it. And when Jimmy Carter became President of the United States, he did, in fact, put a solar water heater on the roof of the White House.

One problem with life is that things don't always work out the way you hope. Another problem with life is that things sometimes do work out the way you hope, and you have to suffer the consequences. It was this second circumstance, after the election of Jimmy Carter in 1976, that was to bring forth my inner gorilla.

Things had seemed so clear and obvious between the time of my solar vision in Miami Beach and the coming of Jimmy Carter to Washington. The Republicans were the bad guys, the friends of Big Oil, who opposed alternative energy development of any kind. Democrats were the good guys and would take commonsense steps to promote solar when they won back the White House.

Democratic pragmatists, I believed, would quickly pass the solar tax credit bill that had first been proposed four years earlier. They would recognize that by making government a major buyer for domestically produced solar water heaters for government buildings, on military installations, and atop post offices, a huge new solar industry would be created on these shores. The White House would also be used as a bully pulpit to encourage homeowners and landlords to buy solar products such as water heaters.

Perhaps in order to get the ball rolling when it came to photovoltaic solar cells, there would also be large orders for such devices to be installed at government installations, thereby bringing down unit costs of this technology and hastening the creation of a market for solar electric as well as for solar water heating products. And in the realm of the purely nitty gritty, local governments would be encouraged to modify their building codes in the scores of little ways that would allow energy direct from the sun to do much of the heating and lighting work being done then by fossil fuels.

That was what I thought would happen. Naif that I was. Because there was no reason, no common sense reason, why it should not happen that way. Being then new to the workings of the American political system, I still believed it operated (at least tangentially) in ways that linked stated goals with the means needed to realize these goals.

What happened instead was this: Fears about future energy shortages leading to perpetual gas lines, fears that Americans would henceforth spend long winter nights bundled in layers of sweaters because they couldn't afford more home heating oil, fears that utilities would run short of fuel and there would be endless brownouts, generated panic in government circles. This, in turn, very quickly brought into being an industry almost as large and even more powerful for a time than the one producing and distributing hydrocarbons — the energy crisis management industry.

This crisis management industry had a huge public component that initially touched virtually every government agency but would ultimately coalesce (or perhaps "clot" is a better word) into a new cabinet level Department of Energy (DOE). It also had a huge private component operating through universities, consulting firms, non-profit agencies and corporate contractors, entities that very quickly became totally dependent on government spending for their incomes, and on government priorities for their own marketing strategies.

Solar, the energy resource, required equipment buyers. Solar, the plaything of a burgeoning policy establishment, needed study and planning, initiatives and interfacing, evaluation and strategizing.

The former atrophied as the latter waxed.

To be fair, the rampant idiocy that was to mark the Carter Administration's own approaches to solar energy had began well before Mr. Carter actually won the White House in 1976. Just 13 days after the start of the Arab-Israeli War of 1973, and almost immediately after the announcement of the Arab Oil Embargo that was an offshoot of this conflict, the National Science Foundation (NSF) announced a big increase in its solar demonstration projects.

A tiny $1.2 million had been allocated to the NSF in 1972 by Congress to do studies about solar energy for the National Aeronautics and Space Administration. In the throes of a post-oil embargo Beltway spasm, this piddling sum was instantly quadrupled. And instead of solar demonstrations in space that were months or even years in the future, high visibility earth-based demonstration projects on public schools were the new order of the day.

To hasten matters further here, NFS staffers dispensed with competitive bidding. Instead they selected some traditional big-name contractors to handle these demonstration projects, though none of these companies had any past experience whatever with solar equipment such as water heaters, unlike some foreign companies long active in the field.

The upshot of such haste and contracting procedures was predictable. One of these school demonstration projects became the subject of a little booklet titled *Hey Dad, Can You Collect*

Solar Energy In The Shade? Another had a projected savings on
energy costs of 845 years.

All these demonstration projects were technical fiascoes. The
people in government who let the contracts were nonetheless
immensely pleased with them because they suggested an ability
to respond quickly in a crisis — rapid response outweighing in
their minds quality of response.

While one group in a befuddled and expiring Gerald Ford
Administration were bungling an early (and with respect to
solar water heaters unnecessary) solar demonstration program,
a far more destructive and far-reaching kind of bungling was
taking place. The Solar Energy Research, Development and
Demonstration Act of 1974 established a set of intellectual
and administrative parameters within which government solar
policies were to flounder for the remainder of the decade.

This act was supposed to encourage "...successful national
research efforts (akin to) the space program and the Manhattan
Project." It called for centrally directed and interrelated efforts
in this regard. It established near-term, mid-term, and long-
term time frames in which various energy technologies were to
become practical and marketable, and operated to see that these
technologies stuck to this predetermined schedule. Since solar
was decreed to have only mid- and long-term priorities by this
act, actions that worked to realize its immediate potential were
ignored, if not actively discouraged.

Such were the hare-brained outlines for a national solar energy
policy that President Jimmy Carter inherited when he came into
office. The aim of getting solar equipment into the hands of
Americans immediately was subordinated to the arrogance of
planners anxious to play at building a twenty-first century solar
future they only sought to realize decades down the road.

President Carter considered these approaches and priorities and found them good. His administration then proceeded to carry them to heights of folly that even in retrospect beggar the imagination.

Federal funding on solar energy had increased almost 100-fold from $1.2 million in 1972 to $114.8 million in 1976, the year President Carter took office. But this was only starters. By 1978 the Carter Administration was spending $415.4 million annually on solar. During his last year in office in 1980, annual spending peaked at $571.1 million.

That year a Department of Energy official was quoted in the Boston Globe saying: "We're so busy trying to shovel solar money out the door, we don't have time to see what happens after it leaves. All the money could be stolen and I wouldn't know it. This place is a madhouse."

"Madhouse" was an accurate description. Much of this effort was gravitating into various high-tech fantasies. The Solar Satellite Power Project, which came to the fore in these years, was a not untypical example of the high-tech genre that appealed to Carter energy planners. Heavily promoted by aerospace contractors and NASA, it called for satellites to sit in synchronous orbit 22,000 miles above the earth and beam back solar power collected in space via low-density microwaves. This plan was alleged to be more efficient than letting solar radiation find its own way to earth without benefit of satellite intermediaries.

For the aquatic-minded, the government spent vast sums

examining the potential of a floating facility that was supposed
to take advantage of the thermal gradient in tropical waters.
For those who preferred their solar dementia played out in
deserts rather than oceans, an enormous power station was to
be constructed in the sand dunes of Southern California, which
would not actually begin producing any power for decades.

As energy became the all pervasive buzz in the Carter years, the
questing beast of functionaries seeking a transcendental meaning
for their otherwise soulless endeavors, the boundless cornucopia
of government largess for the sticky fingered, every new low-
tech and no-tech grant and contract hunter in North America, as
well as their traditional high-tech counterparts, began queuing
up for a place at the solar trough.

There soon ceased to be any meaningful relationship between
federal solar funding and real world solar implementation.
Virtually all activity in this realm became nothing more than a
money grab pitting an established gang of corporate, campus
and consulting interests with their hands long in the government
till, against an upstart gang of environmentalists, community
outreachers and self-proclaimed "consumer protection" types
who wanted a bigger share of the lolly.

It was these latter grant hustlers, the self-proclaimed "consumer
protectors," who were to prove the most insidious and
destructive when it came to undermining near-term solar
acceptance. Only guarantees and warranties of a sort no nascent
industry had ever been required to generate and could possible
afford would satisfy these people when it came to solar heating
equipment.

They created the myth of the "solar fast-buck schemer." These
were supposedly con men preparing to cheat solar equipment
buyers unless such warranties and guarantees were in place — a
process that would take years — and since millions of perfectly
operating solar water heaters were already in place around the

world and had been operating for a very long time were totally unnecessary. The results of such outlandish demands were devastating — though on occasion, painfully funny.

In Massachusetts, for example, where people like myself were desperately trying to create a real world solar market, consumer protectors in the administration of Governor Mike Dukakis (remember him?) actually went so far as to have the state's Solar Action Office placed under the jurisdiction of the state's Office of Consumer Affairs. In terms of shaping the way consumers viewed solar purchases, this was akin to putting a Bureau of Love into the Ministry of Venereal Disease.

Who were these dippy consumer protectors I soon came to regard as the primary threat to the solarization of America? During the 1970's they were mostly bright, young, well-meaning seekers after a new post-civil rights and post-Vietnam War protest cause to fill their days. They became fanatical believers in activist government, incapable of realizing the potential of free markets abetted with just modest and appropriate help from government as the best way to promote solar.

How could you defend yourself from people like this, people who always claimed to be on your side, then did everything possible to scare or otherwise distract paying customers from solar product showrooms with endless warnings about "solar fast-buck schemers?"

Friends like this kill. And kill they did. For all practical purposes the real solar water and space heating market was dead by 1978. Victims of warped government energy policies and the actions of solar's-little-helpers.

I remember an event that took place at Fanueil Hall in Boston
one early summer's day in 1978 that perfectly encapsulated the
craziness of this period. Fanueil Hall is a gloriously historic
and meticulously restored Federalist structure, where over the
course of two centuries many of America's greatest statesmen
have gathered and debated important issues before crowds
of perceptive citizens. This day's solar dog-and-pony show,
however, organized by the Department Of Energy, was a very
different sort of event.

The DOE-boys from Washington had come to bring words
of greeting from the Great Fathers on the Potomac, and to
hear what they endlessly and unctuously referred to as "the
community's" views on how best to promote solar energy. The
community they were here to address bounced and swayed
nervously on the great hall's pew-style benches, or stood
among its Roman pillars gesturing with their placards. It was a
community consisting almost exclusively of solar activists and
solar groupies with no apparent reason for existence other than
to attend events such as this one.

The air was charged with the loose-lipped excitement one finds
in a tightly packed revival tent on a summer's night when a lack
of fresh air and a cloud of floral deodorants combine to mimic
for the desperate to be saved an aura of imminent enlightenment.
Solar acquaintances separated by milling enthusiasts waved at
each other over bobbing heads or happily shook their placards
in greeting. Media types cruised the hall poking tape recorder
mikes into people's faces, or checking the spelling of names that
would appear in the next day's newspapers.

The day's talking parts were played with a predictability that would have done credit to a Moscow show trial. One after another representatives from a plethora of solar organizations, most wearing brightly patterned or richly lettered tie-dyed shirts over jeans, stepped forward to a microphone set up on a table in one aisle of the hall. They identified their group affiliation and made their special pleas to the half-dozen administrators in dark and expensive suits who smiled benignly down on the pleaders from a raised dais.

The feminist movement was gaining political clout at the time, so there were calls for more federally funded women-in-solar seminars. Because aid to the underprivileged had somehow become a dependency of solar energy, more neighborhood-based solar installation training programs was requested — this, though even jobs for existing solar installers had totally dried up. Speaker after speaker, of course, demanded more and better consumer protection.

Then, unexpectedly, a man with a very different set of views seized the microphone. He and I had been sitting next to each other on one of those hard-as-stone Fanueil Hall benches, quietly sharing a good grouse about the proceedings. He was an employee of a solar showroom on Boston's North Shore. I knew him slightly from this work connection.

A few days earlier I had eaten dinner at the home of the showroom's owner. Over a bottle of wine I listened to her sob bitter tears because she was trying so hard, so very hard, to get by. But every time she seemed about to enjoy a sales breakthrough another promised government program that failed to appear, another consumer warning, emptied her store. Soon, she said, she would have to close shop altogether and lay off her help.

Sitting there in Fanueil Hall, among the solar elite, one of her soon-to-be-jobless employees whispered to me: "Are these the biggest assholes you've ever run into in your entire fucking life?"

The biggest? Tough question. Not one that lent itself to a snap judgment. Certainly not without defining terms or setting parameters. "Domestic or foreign," I asked?

"Domestic."

"Are we talking both coasts here? Or just Northeast Corridor?"

My companion leaned closer. "I can't stand these people," he said in a whisper that was slowly rising to conversational decibels, and starting to attract the attention of people around us. "They make my skin crawl. They offend my air. They block out the healing rays of the sun."

He wore a short-sleeve white shirt, buttoned at the throat, and sported a black slim-jim tie that had to be a leftover from his high school graduation. Two blue-black ballpoint pens were in his breast pocket, both of them leaking. He had cigarettes in there, too. A military tattoo adorned one forearm.

He was so wonderfully and remarkable out of place in this setting it made me happy to be alive. I felt like Arlo Guthrie in his Alice's Restaurant incarnation, on the Group W bench among father rapers and Class A litter felons, in a little eddy of sanity surrounded by a frothy sea of madness.

"I gotta say something to these people," my short-sleeved companion squeaked in a voice that had taken on the helium quality that afflicts people when they are suffering grievously at the prospect of getting up in front of an audience, but are steeling themselves to do so anyway. "I gotta."

Suddenly, he was not sitting with me anymore. He was standing in the aisle, holding the audience microphone like a mallet, totally oblivious by virtue of acute speaker's fright to the look of surprise on the face of the woman, half his size, from whom he had snatched the mike.

"Why don't you people stop crapping around!" He croaked. "Why don't you just buy some solar water heaters! Stop talking and buy something!"

That was all he could get out. Even with a full head of anger. Before dropping the microphone back into its holder so awkwardly it fell on the table and began to roll slowly back and forth.

For ten seconds there was a near total silence in the hall. You only heard the static sound produced by a rolling mike. Then, gradually, came a rising and distinctly nasty rustling like rats' feet on ground glass mixed with the buzz of stinging bees whose nest had been poked by a stick. People here and there looked skyward and rolled their eyes in the universal gesture of intellectual disdain. From several quarters the words "Joe Sixpack" were clearly audible. The interloper who had triggered these reactions was now being jostled, tripped, as he tried to return to the seat next to mine. The threat of confrontation was very real.

It was the head DOE-boy on the podium who saved the situation from degenerating into a shouting match, or even worse, an honest debate about overall government solar policies. This fellow had obviously handled scenes like this before during the course of his traveling solar medicine show.

"Thank you for that incisive comment, " he drawled. Everyone in Washington had a little Georgia in his voice that year.

The stirring in the audience ceased. A few people laughed. "May we have another speaker, please?"

The day returned to its pre-ordained business. The interloper was ignored, a certified non-person now. A few people cleared away the unwanted intrusion with a final laugh. "May we have another speaker, please," intoned again the head DOE-boy.

That day I finally understood. My solar dream, a dream of alternative resources making a significant contribution to America's energy mix, would not become a reality now for many years.

Solar's little helpers had won. That was clear. Sol, me, the guy sitting with me on the Group W solar bench, had lost. Something else now beckoned. Payback.

Enter The Gorilla

How could I get back at Them? How could I even the score with a collective so ephemeral as to be almost an abstraction, yet so wired in terms of media and government connections as to be virtually indistinguishable in the public mind from the solar cause? What concrete, what honorable, what non-violent mechanism could be employed to establish myself as real in this sea of suds?

That was the problem that confronted me in the latter part of the 1970s, once it had became painfully obvious that solar was being spiked in the heart by a gaggle of do-gooder sharpies. Part of the solution to this problem arrived in 1978 in the form of gorilla slippers.

It was my birthday. My marriage had broken up a couple of years earlier and I was dating a woman named Marcia. For reasons I now find totally incomprehensible, the birthday present I most wanted that year, most craved, most frequently mentioned to Marcia in the weeks before the big day, was a shoe tree.

It might have been an early symptom of male menopause. Who knows? In any case, Marcia opted to disregard this desire to acquire a wholesome symbol of domestic stodginess and went gift-shopping instead at Jack's Joke Shop in downtown Boston, where she bought me a pair of gorilla slippers.

The things were ugly almost beyond belief. They were really much more undersized shag rugs than shoe clones. Their tops were made of a black woolly material that attracted dirt like a magnet attracts nails, while their soles were made of a thin rubbery material, skin colored, and so flimsy it offered almost no protection against rough surfaces while also being sticky enough to glue you to almost any surface.

Naturally, I immediately fell in love with my new gorilla slippers. Not in any small measure because they provided such a perfect prop for the revenge against solar's little helpers that I had finally decided upon.

For several years, one of the craziest elements in the crippling of solar energy was something called SERI – the Solar Energy Research Institute. The exact genesis of this institution is unclear. But the story making the solar rounds back then was that an aide to Senator Ted Kennedy had gone on a ski vacation in Colorado while Congress was considering the Non-Nuclear Energy R&D Development Act of 1974 and had a brainstorm on the slopes. If there were a Los Alamos of nuclear energy, she reasoned, why not a Los Alamos of solar energy, especially since the Non-Nuclear Development Act likened alternative energy promotion efforts to the Manhattan Project?

Any analogy between promoting nuclear and solar energy was of course totally absurd. A nuclear power plant is huge, complex and potentially highly dangerous, while a solar water heater is just a bucket of fluid with glass on top and piping at the bottom. Cool water enters the bucket, solar radiation trapped by the glass heats this water, which is then piped to a shower or sink. Where is the need for research here? Where is the potential danger to the public?

There's nothing as powerful, however, as a bad idea whose time has come. Especially as this dictum applies to the Congress of the United States of America. Almost as soon as the Non-Nuclear Energy R&D Act was passed by this august body, the competition to get SERI sited in legislators' home districts exploded into a Frankenstein life of its own.

Without even a mission statement, with no ostensible function other than to comply with a line or two in a recently passed piece of legislation, SERI was dubbed by politicians and the national press alike as a critical element in this country's drive for energy independence, and projected to have an annual operating budget in excess of $50 million.

For energy bureaucrats in Washington, spending millions of dollars on an intrinsically worthless and profoundly silly solar research facility presented no problems. How to accommodate the local and regional fund-seeking ghouls who wanted a piece of this action was something else again. Literally hundreds of proposals to site SERI in one part of the country or another, all backed by well-connected Congressmen or other political heavies, flooded the capital.

A Solomon-like solution was clearly required. This took the form of site-ing the main SERI in Golden, Colorado, home of Coors beer, and satellite SERIs in other parts of the country. The one that ended up in Boston was called The Northeast Solar Energy Center, or NESEC for short. It was organized as a private corporation receiving federal funding for its operations.

NESEC became my gorilla target of choice, the formal beginning of my decades-long crusade against appendages of public and private bureaucratic idiocy. I reasoned that just fighting against "the system" or battling "policy" was ultimately a waste of time. To be effective one had to be more focused.

So I decided to select one institution. Just one. NESEC. And clobber it into non-existence.

My inspiration for this approach was a line about confronting evil from *The Devil And Daniel Webster,* that wonderful play of Archibald Macleish, based on a story by Stephen Vincent Benet. To paraphrase this line: If one Massachusetts man couldn't still beat the devil, even in 1978, what was this country coming to?

The challenge here proved less daunting than first appearances might suggest. The Northeast Solar Energy Center at its peak had about a hundred employees and a budget of several million dollars. I worked alone and was more or less indigent. But I had shorter interior lines of communication, a sense of humor, and the gift of literacy.

All things considered, it was a pretty fair fight.

Atlantic Avenue was then a sliver of Boston's commercial district abutting Boston Harbor and separated from the rest of city by an eight-lane expressway. NESEC had its headquarters on Atlantic Avenue. The easiest way to reach it from the center of town was to walk across a footbridge that had been erected over the highway. It was here I struck my first blows.

I had a flyer printed up containing the case against NESEC. Then waited for nightfall.

With the coming of darkness I slipped on a black sweater, a black hood, and Marcia's black-topped gorilla slippers, and drove to the city side of the Atlantic Street overpass. Moving stealthily between parked cars, ducking in and out of darkened building entrance ways, I waited for the bridge to clear of foot traffic. Then I raced up its stairs and along its length, plastering every post and pillar along the way with my flyers. I made it back to my car before anyone could stop and question the hooded gorilla.

Early the next morning I was back at the bridge, watching the reaction to my plastering job. It was better than I could have imagined.

A few early arriving office workers stopped on the bridge to read my stuff and laughed as they went on their way. Other passers-by, who I recognized as NESEC employees, were much less pleased by what they saw. They ripped down some of the flyers. About an hour after NESEC office hours officially started a small squad of them were on the bridge tearing them all down and combing the area for possible other postings.

I had learned NESEC's fatal weakness. Fear of a bad public image. And I knew I owned them.

Like mushrooms, bad bureaucratic edifices grow best where the light is poorest. This is what made my particular mode of criticism so dangerous to these shadow-lovers. The thing under attack was not the unreachable "government" or a generic "government policy." I was focusing negative attention on a single easily identifiable government appendage that might, by virtue of being spotlighted, get the axe first when the inevitable solar funding mania ended.

That great American political philosopher, Deep Throat, said it all when he said, "follow the money." By threatening NESEC's future funding I was aiming for the institution's heart. Its purse.

I conducted dozens of broad sheet raids wearing gorilla slippers on NESEC headquarters in Boston. Sometimes late at night. Sometimes in broad daylight. Sometimes on weekends. They brought much needed attention to the organization and were lots of fun in the bargain.

This work was supplemented by stamping and stickering. I had a hand stamper made up with the words "The New England Solar Energy Center must be destroyed." It was not only used on all my own mailings, but once or twice was slipped to a malcontent in NESEC's own mailroom. He applied it to every letter coming in the morning mail, suggesting a widely orchestrated campaign.

The stickers I used were those little things one puts on envelopes in the self-address part. I printed up thousands of them with the same "NESEC must be destroyed" wording and posted them everywhere. On public telephones. Above urinals and on the mirrors in restrooms. On the counters of pubs and on chairs in restaurants. On parking meters. Pretty soon a lot in people in Boston were wondering who or what was a NESEC, and why did it have to be destroyed.

I wrote dozens of articles in the local and national press under my own name criticizing NESEC. I also acted as a conduit directing negative information about the center to other journalists, many of whom by this time were waking up to the fact that solar the ideal had degenerated into solar the honey pot.

These activities, of course, very quickly attracted the attention of the folks who ran NESEC. More importantly, word of my existence filtered down to the organization's non-executive cadre, many of whom were not happy campers. They might not share my goal to destroy an organization that provided them with a paycheck, but because they were refugees from a solar equipment and installation marketplace the government's warped policies had undermined while pumping up their present employer, they were more than happy to at least help me make their bosses miserable by feeding me embarrassing internal tidbits.

For two years, off-and-on, sometimes in highly concentrated spurts lasting a week or two, sometimes with a month or two between gorilla raids, I went after my target. This wasn't a personal vendetta against anyone in particular within the organization. It wasn't done in the belief that NESEC was the worst solar perversion in the country. It was simply in pursuit of the idea that something worthwhile had to be avenged, a statement made, and only an outsider with a rep, a passion, a focus, and a sense of humor could do the job.

Only once during this period did I have actual contact with NESEC's chief, a former consultant, Larry L. And this encounter was a tad unusual to say the least —though from a gorilla perspective it made perfect sense.

At the time I was living in a part of Boston called Jamaica Plain. There were no large supermarkets near my apartment building, so I had to drive to a large grocery store near the old Fenway Park where the Boston Braves baseball team used to play. Across the street from this store was a restaurant with some very large windows facing out on the street.

It was about six o'clock one evening in summer, the light was still very good, I was leaving the market with my groceries when I happened to look across the street and saw Larry at a window table of this restaurant. He was dining alone and seemed lost in thought.

It was a magnificent opportunity, one too good to pass up. I raced to my car and stashed the groceries in its back seat. From the trunk, where I always stocked anti-NESEC flyers, I selected an especially garish canary yellow number and a roll of tape. Then I took up a position where I could see Larry clearly from behind a tree, but couldn't be seen by him. And waited.

Luck was with me that evening. Larry got up from his table a few moments later to go to the washroom. Racing across the street, I taped a gorilla flyer on the window right next to his table, facing inward, and got back to my stake-out position behind the tree.

I watched as he returned. He noticed the flyer immediately. He stared at it, long and hard. Then looked around the restaurant, out the restaurant's window, straining to glimpse something, anything, that would explain what was happening to him and to his organization. Then stared at the flyer again. Long and hard.

Poor Larry. He left the restaurant without finishing his meal.

Something happened in the years I was doing the gorilla with solar energy. Something that could possibly be explained as just a series of unlikely coincidences, but which struck me then, and still strikes me today, as bordering on the preternatural.

My marriage had ended. My work with solar, now pretty much a full-time job, paid very little. Inside the mad solar loop the money flowed freely. Pointing out the loop's idiocy garnered peanuts. It was easy to get depressed. I got depressed.

One good thing in this period was that I had joint custody of my son. When it was my time to care for him, I would pick him up at his mother's place near the Fresh Pond section of Cambridge.

One day when I came by there, he was delayed at school and I had some time on my hands. I walked a couple of blocks and came to a small bookstore. Though I had lived with my ex-wife in this neighborhood for years, I had never visited this book store. This one time I did.

There were books on shelves in the front, but for some reason I walked to the rear where there were stacks of assorted magazines. I picked one up at random. It just happened to be Solar Age, a magazine I sometimes wrote for.

This issue of Solar Age I held in my hands didn't contain one of my articles. It was the issue after one of my pieces had appeared. Perusing, I opened it, again at random, and came to the letters page. And there was a letter from someone in far off Kansas writing that my piece in the previous issue opened her eyes and changed the way she looked at energy and the future generally.

A store I'd never visited before. A magazine picked at random that sometimes ran my articles. Its letter page stumbled upon with a missive from a perfect stranger saying my work had changed the way she looked at the future.

It could have been a lot of coincidences. I thought otherwise. I was being sent a message. Tilt against that windmill some more.

So I did.

In 1980 it was finally end game. Time to bury NESEC. Time to finish my own gorilla war against that organization.

Ronald Reagan had just been elected President. A god-awful happening for the country, certainly, but something that fit nicely with my own gorilla agenda.

I asked a friend at the Boston Globe what single media exposure would guarantee that NESEC would get the budgetary axe faster than anything else. "Stick it to 'em on the Op Ed page of the New York Times," he replied. Which is what I did.

On Wednesday, December 10, 1980, about a month after Ronald Reagan's election, a piece of mine headed "Reagan And Solar Energy" appeared in that newspaper of record. One reason this piece is a personal favorite of mine is the other writers on that day's Times' Op Ed page — Russell Baker, then-Illinois Senator Adelai E. Stevenson, and James Reston, a trio with whom I had absolutely no business sharing this space except that sometimes The Force truly is with you. In an equally satisfying vein this piece succeeded in terminating my chosen foe.

Within the context of a general critique of Carter solar energy policy I mentioned that the head of one government-supported solar outpost (Larry of NESEC) was getting a salary larger than that of the President of the United States.

Bye-bye Larry. Bye-bye NESEC. Both were defunded, I believe, sooner than any other major government supported solar enterprise.

After my piece appeared in the New York Times I got a call from
the producer of public television's MacNeil-Lehrer Report. She
invited me to be on the show that night to discuss the future of
solar energy in the wake of a Reagan election win.

I said no. In part, because I thought it was pretty high-handed to
expect someone to show up at a television station on such short
notice. Gorillas aren't media pets. We just use media as needed.
Beyond that, after long years in this game, I felt that I'd done all
that I had to do with respect to solar energy and it was time to
move on.

Gorilla postscripts.

Did my gorilla work on behalf of the great star Sol over a
period of almost seven years have any lasting value in actually
solarizing America? Not really. Measured as a purely activist
effort to realize a major change, it was just a very minor puff of
air directed against a very strong Establishment headwind with
utterly predicable non-results.

In my swansong effort as a solar gorilla, my Op Ed piece in The
New York Times, I wrote: "Given the nature of past Federal
Government efforts in the solar field, Mr. Reagan's activities
would almost certainly have to be an improvement…his
statements about excessive Government spending indicate that
he will do away with the most blatant examples of waste here…
Thus, the Reagan Administration will be a boon to the real solar

industry, though it may well devastate the phony solar industry that sells paper to the Department of Energy..."

Of course, I was dead wrong in this prediction, as wrong in my expectations for a new Reagan Administration when it came to promoting solar properly as I had been with a new Carter Administration. President Reagan was a complete bust when it came to advancing solar and alternative energy generally. His energy policies were almost totally oil-based and oil enhancing. In an egregiously nasty swipe at his predecessor, Mr. Reagan even had the solar heater atop the White House removed.

Neither Democratic nor Republican administrations that followed were much better from a solar perspective. There have been many unfortunate results in consequence. Perhaps the most obvious one involves China.

In the 1970s the United States had the technology base, the resources, a large and willing potential market, everything needed to immediately create the largest, most profitable, most job-producing solar industry in the world, one that would also become the prime exporter of these technologies to the rest of the world. What we got instead was a classic example of how government should not operate, a continued dependence on fossil fuels, and the chance to watch the Chinese eat our solar lunch and become the world's major supplier of solar products.

Today solar, wind, geothermal and other alternative energy technologies are finally finding a major place in this country's overall energy mix. Even so, because of a failure of vision at the top of our society, an obvious truth is still not appreciated nor appropriately promoted.

That truth: Live, natural, abundant, and eternal energy resources are an inherently better way to animate a human economy than raiding the burial grounds of long dead plants and animals to garner fossil fuels to do the job.

Sadly, in terms of making this transformation happen sooner, or its implications clearer, I was a failure. But there was a personal upside. In terms of my personal development, doing what I did for solar was a truly transformative experience.

I was still a passive chimp when I got back from Miami in 1973. By the time I got that Op Ed in The New York Times in 1980 I'd become a full-fledged gorilla.

I was ready for the next opportunity to rattle other establishment cages.

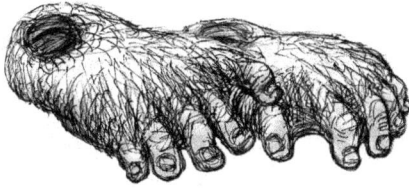

II
Looking Backwards:
A Pre-Gorilla Grows In Brooklyn

What prepared me for the gorilla gambit described above, and the other gorilla campaigns described later in this book? What events in my early life set the tone and gave me an outlook on life that led me to take the gorilla road?

My earliest recollections are of watching ChiChi Semoni shooting passersby in the ass with his BB gun, and his demented brother, Bobby Semoni, having head fights with an even more demented Robert Mundy in the hallway of our five-story apartment building on West 5th Street in Bensonhurst in the borough of Brooklyn, New York. It was 1949 and I was eight years old.

These were amazingly good times for most Americans. Indeed, in many ways, the acme of American civilization. We had just whipped the Nazis and were standing up to the Commies. We were consuming 60 percent of a post-WWII world's total goods and services and feeling no qualms about doing so. Almost any American could buy a two-bedroom house with a yard for $9,000 or $10,000, no down payment, four percent mortgage, no credit check. You only had to work 40 hours a week to enjoy an ever growing pile of goodies, and only one member of the household had to work outside the home to get them.

If you lived in Manhattan things were often even better. In spite of whines and snivels from far-away Europeans, it was pretty clear to almost everyone that Manhattan had become the center of Western culture, and at least for a time, world culture.

It was a time when immigrant German-Jewish music teachers could afford to live in huge rent-controlled apartments on Manhattan's West End Avenue and regularly attend operas at the Met, standing room, for a buck. If you were young and a veteran with no means of support but GI benefits, you could still afford the rent on a downtown apartment, pay your college tuition, and work writing an awful war novel. With luck you could also get laid in Greenwich Village fairly often with girls wearing green stockings and berets if you could put up with the quirky political bullshit that passed for foreplay in those days.

Of course, only a trickle of the excitement and opportunities represented by these impossibly favorable and inherently short-lived circumstances penetrated my own tightly knit Jewish and Italian enclave in the Bensonhurst section of Brooklyn. This was Saturday Night Fever country before anyone had gotten the fever. A big unmelted pot of insecure ethnicity, filled with angry people who hadn't made it big enough to move to Long Island and who couldn't cut it across the river in Manhattan. A kind of ultra-claustrophobic, working class, lefty-cum-Roosevelt-community of automatic Democratic lever pullers. It was the kind of insular place where a kid like me could get half-way through adolescence without suspecting that not all Italians were Sicilians, and not all Christians were Catholics.

On the upside, though, you couldn't beat some of the local entertainment. Like the way ChiChi ran his shooting gallery.

He and his younger brother Bobby lived in a basement apartment with a hard-drinking building superintendent father whose idea of plumbing was to beat the crap out of the basement boiler pipes with a huge wrench, and a mother who didn't speak English but was nonetheless able to communicate strong opinions with extraordinary clarity using fingers that could bend into configurations you hated to think might ever find their way into places her gestures suggested she meant to put them.

ChiChi did his BB shooting with a Red Rider air rifle, single shot, western pump model, from behind the hinged-at-the-top window of the basement apartment where the Semonis lived next to the boiler. The game was played while his folks were out and with his little bother Bobby nearby, goading him on.

ChiChi would nail an empty wallet to the sidewalk across the street, wait for an unsuspecting pedestrian to bend over to pick it up, then pop him in the ass when he did. The victim, of course, spun around in the direction of our five-story apartment building. But by then the Semoni boys had let the hinged basement window flap shut and were ducked out of sight.

A few of us usually watched this drama from the building's roof and jeered at the discomfort and confusion on view in the street below. Sometimes we even joined the fun by tossing down water-filled balloons that splattered on the street like huge explosive raindrops. A pained victim of this youthful urban exuberance sometimes seemed inclined to go after his tormentors, but invariably thought better of the idea. The half-dozen lightly armed Bart Simpsons he could see, and the shooters he could not see but knew were lurking nearby, hinted at even more lethal horrors waiting in this Bensonhurst Thunderdome.

ChiChi was wild, but you figured the Marine Corps or Attica would settle him out. His brother Bobby didn't have that kind of promise. The kid was burdened down with funny looks, bad breath, low intelligence, and arms that hung down long enough to sport roller skates. He also preferred his conflict close, flesh and bone touching, not BB shot length.

Bobby had a hate thing going with my own best friend in those years, Robert Mundy. Nobody knew why. They could have been twins the way they looked. Squat, dark complexioned, perpetually unkempt hair, snot-coated shirt sleeves, fingers gooed with the same substance. They thought alike, too, though neither was really big on thinking. They were emoters, actors out, the kind of perpetually over-excited and prone to violence kids that today would be lunching from the tranquilizer cabinet in the school nurse's office from their first day in kindergarten.

The animosity between Bobby and Robert found its fullest expression in their regular head fights, which took place in the building's narrow ground floor hallways. Here the illumination was provided by weak overhead bulbs and the walls were painted the color of liberty ships. Here people dripped grease and maybe worse from the bottom of brown paper bags they carried on the way to garbage cans that were always out in front of the building because the super was too drunk or lazy to bring them inside between pick-up days.

These epic struggles would begin when Bobby and Robert took their usual positions on either end of the musty, ill-lit, bowling lane-shaped hallway arena. There would be a minute or two of traded insults. Then they charged each other.

You could hear the collision a block away. Neither of the combatants ever went down, however. Both merely snorted, let their heads roll loosely back and forth a few times to clear the cobwebs and maybe try to remember who they were and what the hell they were fighting about, before ambling back to their starting positions preparing to do it again. Naturally, these battles attracted the building's other youthful delinquents, who would look down at the contest while sitting on stairwell steps or peering over the railings on higher floors.

It was usually after the second or third head bashing that Yetta Mundy, Robert's mother, came storming down from her second floor apartment, brushing aside or stepping over those of us on the staircase who had come to watch the fun. Nobody, of course, obstructed her passage. You'd be insane to try. The Mundys had changed their family name from Mundamensky in order to better meld into American society, but the transformation in Yetta's case was only name deep. She remained a pure breed Polish-Jewish ghetto beserker.

Furious at her son's behavior, his fighting with a super's kid in a public hallway within hearing of respectable neighbors, and with a cheering section of local children looking on no less, Yetta stormed toward the head fighters like a crazed wigged Buddha until she stood over them, shaking with anger. Then, instead of exploding into foreign shouts and vicious slaps—the favored child-rearing method of most other local crazies who occasionally intervened to stop a head fight—Yetta stuck one of her wrists into her own mouth. Deep into her mouth, and bit down so hard that the blood gushed. It was the dreaded Yetta Mundy Wrist Chomp.

Her eyes got wider and wider the deeper her teeth sunk into the flesh of her goose-necked wrist until you could almost hear the capillaries popping. And as she devoured herself in this masochistic spasm, this extraordinary maternal expiation of her son's social shame, her eyes would roll like black marbles and her head would sway in a kind of singsong agony. Her feet eventually got into the act, too, stamping out a kind of troll's jig. She looked like a blood-pricked frog on a scalding fry pan.

Even a Semoni, steeped in lurid Sicilian family tales of stiletto assassinations and vendettas carried on with sawed off shotguns, was cowed into silence by the sight of the Yetta Mundy Wrist Chomp. After a few horrified and speechless seconds, Bobby Semoni would back away slowly, turn, and not look back while rapidly exiting the building's front door. Robert Mundy would start after him, giving his departing foe a finger of triumph, but never got very far before his ear was seized by the hand Yetta didn't still have wedged in her teeth and he was pulled upstairs for further discussions.

How could you not love people like this? How could witnessing behavior like this fail to leave you believing that human kind is irredeemably silly?

Of course, the ethnic craziness in this neighborhood wasn't always as silly and life affirming as the Yetta Mundy variety. Nor did it always just produce relatively non-lethal concussions and badly chewed wrists. The man who taught Sunday morning classes at the synagogue I attended for bar mitzvah lessons was Rabbi Meir Kahane, founder of the Jewish Defense League.

I had a good seat in these classes, first row left, and was able to experience the man close up. His pulpy lips, pockmarked complexion. His oily black hair topped by a yarmulke held in place with bobby pins. His egregiously nasty religious chauvinism and rabid militancy. His version of Jewish morality encapsulated in a phrase he was fond of using: "After Auschwitz, no one can tell us we can't do anything."

Even as a 12-year-old I knew this guy was a real schmuck.

I nonetheless went out of my way never to miss one of these classes because of the girl sitting behind me there. Naomi. She played a leading role in my fantasy world at the time, a time when America was also deep in a Cold War with Russia and regular take-cover drills were part of every school curriculum.

In one of these fantasies I was walking near my home when I happened to look up and saw the unmistakable red star on the fuselage of a Russian bomber flying directly overhead. Just then it opened its bomb bay and nuclear mega-death was sent plunging toward my street in Bensonhurst.

I knew what I had to do. What any real American kid in that era knew he had to do. I leaped on the bomb as it hit the ground and absorbed the blast with my own body.

A tough way to go, sure. But at least I'd saved Naomi.

Little did I realize back then that the kind of heroic masochism in this daydream would so often be on view in my future real life.

III.
Parking Capers
(A Ticked Off Gorilla Motorist Strikes Back)

On December 16, 1773, some citizens of Boston got dressed up as Mohawk Indians and dumped a load of tea in Boston Harbor. This wonderfully staged bit of political theater, which marked a critical milestone on the road to a full-blown American Revolution, was both a big issue protest against taxation without representation and an angry response to a toll on a local addiction—tea drinking.

My own gorilla work against excessive parking ticketing in Boston more than two centuries later had similar motives. The big issue was the sneaky way the Boston City government was levying taxes. My angry response also reflected the fact that one group of citizens—car-addicted folks like myself—were being singled out for a screwing.

Parking tickets are indeed a tax. A curb tax. And unlike other taxes imposed by local governments, the size of this exaction and the way it's collected aren't directly determined by elected representatives who must bear the political consequences.

If a local government wants to raise property taxes, the mayor, the city council, or some other person or group of elected officials has to propose the hike publicly and take the heat.

Boosting the take from parking tickets only requires changing the way some existing parking regulations are enforced. The increased revenue that results from predatory enforcement can then be billed as 'a crackdown on scofflaws' rather than a boost in the local tax rate.

Another attractive feature of parking tickets (attractive, that is, from the collectors' perspective) is that this is a mosquito tax. When a local government sticks it to property owners, the hit comes in hefty quarterly or annual bites. A parking ticket, like a mosquito, sucks up just a little at a time. It's annoying, yes, but rarely annoying enough to cause organized opposition, even when the bite is repeated endlessly.

Over time smart public officials also learn to reduce animosity toward their curb taxes by training ticket issuers to be more courteous, by forgiving some tickets if motorists take the time and trouble to protest them, and by making fine paying easier. Cash? Check? Debit card? Master Card? Visa? No problem. Have a nice day.

It's only in the first year or two after a local government decides to make a serious effort to turn its curbs into toll booths and unleash on an unsuspecting public a gang of ambulatory revenue enhancers disguised as meter maids that feelings are raw enough to make gorilla activity in this field worthwhile. I happened to be in Boston when that city took the plunge.

In 1981 Boston collected just $1.2 million in parking fines. By 1985 that figure had risen to $34 million—a figure equal to $54 for every man, women, and child then living in the city.

The motoring public cried for relief. That didn't happen. But at least it did get a gorilla response.

In the early 1980's I was living in the Jamaica Plain section of Boston. J.P. as everyone called it. A place that Walter Mondale carried nine-to-one in the presidential election of 1984 while Ronald Reagan was trouncing him most everywhere else in the country.

J.P. was a place you could love.

Kay, my ultra significant other, had appeared in my life by then, and on summer evenings we would join the lines at JP Licks, the local ice cream emporium. The wait was always long, but the conversations you heard were so interesting the time seemed to fly by. This was due in large measure to the fact that everyone on the line, including Kay and myself, was stoned out of our gourds.

"The peach melba is good, man. Really, really good," one of the patiently waiting crowd might intone.

"I don't deny that," someone else would answer. "But I'm tellin' you, you gotta try the pistachio supreme. I hit a patch of pistachio in my last cone and saw God."

"Cones? Cones? What's all this shit with cones?" another voice entered the fray. "It's cups, man. You gotta get yourself into a cup frame of consciousness."

At this juncture there would be a group dialogue pitting cups against cones. Until one determined speaker would pipe up: "Are you cup people crazy? Cups and cones are the same price. But you can't eat a cup."

"I eat my cups," replied someone further down the line.

"Alright. Look. I'm not saying there's anything wrong with eating plastic cups. This is a free country. Am I right?"

"Right on," responded several people on the line who had been following the argument (if that's what it was) closely. "But you get more ice cream in cones," this speaker continued. "It's simple physics, man. It's the way they pack the ice cream down into the cone. You get a squash effect."

"Right on," chimed in the chorus. "Right on."

Yes, those were days when people took their ice cream seriously. Indeed, I had my own gorilla-like apotheosis while devouring a JP Licks double rich vanilla cone.

I owned an old Volkswagen at the time. It couldn't pass inspection because there was a crack in the windshield, So here I was, licking this double rich vanilla ice cream while thinking about the cracked windshield that I couldn't afford to replace. And it suddenly occurred to me that if I covered the crack in my car's windshield with some double rich vanilla ice cream it would look exactly like bird shit, and no inspector is going to take the trouble to wipe it off.

Which is how I got the car past inspection. Which is how I was able to drive it around Boston and its environs. Which is why I got caught up in the city's parking ticket blitz.

While anger about this municipal tax scam was just beginning to percolate, I went to get a haircut at a neighborhood barbershop. It was one of those establishments where the cutters weren't all that obsessive when it came to cleaning their scissors between clients, but compensated by charging less than ten bucks a visit. I figured the danger of coming home with something I don't like was minimal because I was almost bald on top anyway.

I also liked the fact that these shops have old hunting and fishing magazines in their waiting areas, thereby saving me the trouble of actually hunting or fishing. I liked the spinning candy stick poles in their front windows. I liked the Korean War-vintage chairs with metal rod legs and plastic seat covers that make bathroom noises when you shift your weight around on the barber chair.

The barber who trimmed my residual side hairs in J.P. in the early 1980s, however, happened not to be the usual elderly Italian male. She was a young woman, puffy-faced, frizzy-haired, round-shouldered, always tired looking, a good listener who didn't say much herself. That is until during one of my regular ten-dollar (with the tip thrown in) visits I happened to mention that I'd just gotten my third parking ticket in as many days. She exploded.

After putting in a hard fifty-hour week she liked to unwind by hitting the bars down by the waterfront. And every time she'd done this in the last few months she'd gotten hit with parking tickets. Not the eight-dollar numbers I had received in recent days either. Her's were whopping twenty-five dollar shaftings.

"I'm paying a third of my income now in parking tickets," she said, livid. The scissors hissed. I began to fear for my ears.

"What am I supposed to do?" she continued angrily. "Not go out for a few pops on the weekend? What kind of friggin' town is this getting to be? You want that cut round or square in the back, honey?"

It suddenly came to me. My barber was another Murray Garfunkel. She was letting me know that an idea that had been percolating in my head, a gorilla action against the local parking authority, was not just a personal crackpot venture (though that would be OK, too), but another worthwhile battle on my personal gorilla agenda.

I found excessive parking ticketing in Boston and its environs during the early 1980s objectionable not only because it was a sneaky tax. It was also a symptom of the changing culture in the town I'd hoped would always be my hometown.

After being fired from a job in New York City I went with my wife at the time and my very young son Jon to Nantucket, where we lived during the Island's off-season (back then it had an off-season from the end of Labor Day to Memorial Day). We then came to Cambridge, Massachusetts and found a great rental near Harvard Square. When my marriage broke up, I moved across the river to the Jamaica Plain section of Boston.

Boston-Cambridge when I first arrived here was a wonderfully funky, down-at-the-heels, cheap and cheeky sort of place. A northeastern city gone to seed, but one that was also richly enlivened by the intellectualism that oozed copiously from its famous educational facilities, enlivened by competing Irish and Brahmin political structures, home to a life-enhancing assortment of other ethnic crazies and perpetual students.

The place overflowed with happily stoned, over-sexed, well-meaning drop-outs and fades-outs who had largely escaped the pile-on-the-goods-and-services mania that had so warped their parents' lives and was beginning to warp the lives of so many of their peers elsewhere in the country.

By the time I left Boston in the late 1980s, however, it had been taken over by lawyers and free market hustlers. Real estate was so gentrified you had to work twenty more hours a week just to afford the same place you used to inhabit for a song before they installed new locks and buffed up the hardwood floors. Everything looked brighter, cleaner, more sterile, more grown up, deadly serious.

Underpaid restaurant help had learned to serve as though it mattered, instead of as if you were both sharing a rather silly commercial joke. Cops called you 'sir' or 'ms' while writing out speeding tickets. A kind of universal camaraderie based on nobody going anywhere and certainly not going there in a hurry had been replaced by sharp class lines based on a flood of new funny money.

The population was becoming what deToqueville termed "industrious sheep," a disease that many of us in the 1960s and early 1970s hoped had been eradicated forever on these shores. Boston-Cambridge had morphed into another post-Maggie Thatcher London, a Singapore on the Charles.

The parking revolution, I was to chronicle in partnership with my now life mate, Kay Wood, and for a brief moment disrupt in this urban setting, was part of this god-awful transformation. Society's new elite had decreed that we would all now honor our leaders and pay our parking meters—or else. The vastly expanded parking ticketing that resulted, they claimed, would expedite vehicular movement, improve air quality, facilitate business, and ratchet up local bond ratings. Copiously issued and efficiently collected parking tickets would be another visible and outward sign of the "world class city" they so desired.

I don't like world class. It smelled then, it smells worse now. Smells of a deep income-based split in society. I didn't like the smell of world class ticketing in Boston. So I set about learning more about parking meters and the horrors they spawned in preparation for another gorilla strike.

Perhaps the first mention in literature of ticketing related to driving was in Jacques Futrelle's 1905 short story, "The Phantom Motor." Set in the County of Yarborough in England, it contains these lines: "...the county was particular about its [motor car] speed laws, so particular in fact that it had stationed half a hundred men on its highways to abate the nuisance. Incidentally, it had found that keeping record of the infractions of the law was an excellent source of income."

The other kind of ticketing, for vehicles that were parked rather than moving, has a history in this country that only really goes back to 1935. That was when parking meters first appeared in Oklahoma City, the brainchild of a reporter named Carl Magee. When the first batch of meters was installed, people came from miles around to the unveiling and to try one out. One of these original meters is now on display at the Oklahoma Historical Society.

Heavy reliance on parking meters, parking ticketing, resident parking sticker fees, towing, and all the other curb tax-related gimmicks employed by local government officials tends to be cyclical. Such revenues helped many cities and towns get through the financially troubled Depression. In flush times, though, this revenue 'resource' tends not to be pursued very aggressively.

The biggest opposition to over-zealous ticketing in prosperous post-WW II America often came from city merchants. The malls springing up in suburbs were sapping the retail appeal of downtowns, and malls offered acres of free parking. Ticketing shoppers who still ventured into the downtown didn't strike city storeowners as a very good idea. They leaned on big city administrations and parking ticketing faded for a time.

Many smaller municipalities dropped out of the parking ticket business for another reason. Their older meters, which only accepted pennies and nickels, cost more to keep in service than they generated in income.

Parking ticketing in all its guises resurfaced strongly even before energy-based hard times hit city and town budgets hard in the 1970s. The soon to become toxic relationship between local governments increasingly meter-addicted and their citizens was made clear in the 1967 movie "Cool Hand Luke." After Paul Newman, the film's hero, decapitated a Duncan parking meter, he was first sent him to the slammer and ultimately assassinated by local constabulary.

By the 1970s no one would dare challenge the right of cities and towns so directly when it came to curbside toll collections. The curb tax had again become a favorite revenue enhancer around the country.

New York, which had the largest numbers of meters of any American city (68,000), led the way in seeking extra income from its curb tax. Fiscally speaking it had little choice. The city was so tapped out by the mid-1970's that its budgeting and spending were taken over by The New York State Financial Control Board. Control by this state agency explains why tickets

issued in The Apple were the first to include a state surcharge of
$5.

It's one thing to issue parking tickets, of course, and another
to collect on them. At one time New York was owed 1.1
billion dollars in unpaid parking fines. It was seeking to boost
collections on unpaid tickets that led New York City to make one
of its most important contributions to the curb tax revolution—
turning administration of the system over to private companies
in 1974.

In this regard it's worth remembering that the practice of
letting private parties collect debt owed to governments is
called 'tax farming,' and tax farming has a long and tainted
history of breeding corruption and ill-will. The publicans in the
bible, Rome's private tax collectors, are portrayed as the most
debased of men and those in greatest need of redemption. Alexis
DeToqueville is just one of the historians to place much of the
blame for the French Revolution on the private tax gatherers
employed by the French monarchy.

Overdue parking tickets were the first modern public debt that
private parties collected for any U.S. government—federal, state
or local—since the Civil War when Mr. Lincoln's Administration
was so financially strapped it briefly employed this tactic. Today,
alas, many local governments in this country allow these private
ghouls to collect a variety of public debt.

New York wasn't the only major city whose economic woes
in the 1970s led to a growing dependence on the curb tax. The
Philadelphia parking story is in many ways as poignant—and
instructive.

Philadelphia's Traffic Court long heard parking ticket-
related cases and excused the fines of more than 80 percent
of complaining motorists. After the Traffic Court's ticketing
functions were given to a city agency, the Finance Department,

just 23 percent of cases were excused and another 13 percent of fines reduced. Collections blossomed.

Liberating the ticketing system from protections offered an accused by courts is a necessity for any local government wishing to really collect big on its parking tickets. This necessity was addressed in Boston even earlier than in Philadelphia.

In 1981 the Massachusetts legislature decreed that Boston city courts would no longer adjudicate ticketing disputes. The fact that you got a ticket now proved you deserved it. The only way this law allowed you to beat the rap was if you could present "credible and sufficient" evidence that you didn't deserve the ticket, and this evidence had to be "documentary."

So much for due process. So much for the right to face your accuser. So much for the presumption of innocence until proven guilty.

Not surprisingly, with this generous assistance from the Massachusetts legislature, Boston's parking ticket collection rate soon became the highest in the nation. By the end of the 1980's the city was collecting fines on about 85 percent of the tickets it issued. New York, by way of contrast, collected on about 50 percent. Philadelphia was right in the middle, collecting on about 72 percent.

Naturally there's another side to the curb tax issue. The number of legal public parking spaces in Boston where I was living in the early 1980s was capped at 35,000 by the federal Environmental Protection Agency because of pollution worries. This brought about a greater need to turn over a limited number of parking spaces in a geographically small city. Ticketing does this, and also promotes mass transit, which is good thing, too.

Any fair-minded person would carefully consider arguments on both sides before making any final judgments about curb taxes, much less taking action in this field. But I'm not a fair-minded person. I'm a gorilla. And in all honesty, Boston's parking authorities in these years were not only greedy and sneaky, they were frequently cruel and callous.

One example. In 1982 a car was towed away with a dog inside while the dog's owner was having lunch. The car had some unpaid tickets. The dog ended in the pound and was put down before the owner could rescue his vehicle.

In 1984 a man died of a heart attack while parked in a car in the Back Bay section of Boston. The vehicle was tagged with five parking tickets before someone bothered to call an ambulance. That someone wasn't the meter maid who issued the tickets.

Barber abuse! Pet abuse! Dissing a corpse! These aren't the kind of things a chimp, much less a gorilla, takes in stride.

I'm no dummy. I know you can't beat city hall. Still, you take your whacks and sometimes you lands a lucky punch.

John Hersey is best known for his journalistic masterpiece, *Hiroshima*, and for his novels, *A Bell For Adano* and *The Wall*. My own favorite piece of Hersey's writing, though, is a little remembered novella titled *My Petition For More Space*.

It's set in a nameless time and place where people are living in very cramped and crowded circumstances, a time and place ruled over by persons (or perhaps they are machines) never actually seen. The only hope for improved conditions for people living here is to line up for a hearing on matters such as a petition for more personal space. These requests are made through a mirrored surface that doesn't allow one to see the party on the other side.

None of these requests is ever granted. Petitioning is thus a kind of masochistic game—asking again and again for piddling favors in slightly different ways without a rational hope of ever getting a positive response.

A similar ambiance pervaded the place in Boston where motorists went in the early 1980's to petition for a break on improperly issued parking tickets. While the people screwing over you in Boston were certainly human, their treatment of petitioners was no more humane.

In the first few months after the ferocious new Boston curb tax regime came into effect, people petitioning for parking ticket relief came to the fourth floor of City Hall. As one got off the elevator there, a policewoman with an oversized firearm on her ample hip and a 'don't try anything funny' expression handed you a card explaining why you were almost certainly wasting your time. Card in hand, you then walked a few steps and were at the end of a long waiting line.

There were only a few plastic chairs here. Most people had to stand. By mid-morning the area's two undersized public restrooms were clogged. Water from a single drinking fountain rose a mere inch or two above its round metal cap, bestowing an indirect kiss from the other hundred people who used it before you took your own turn.

This was an era when smoking was still permitted in public buildings and the hallway reeked of tobacco. Dust motes danced in a blue-white cigarette haze. Hacking coughs barked at you like dogs in a kennel. "Fucking assholes..." and "I gotta get back to work..." and "I know a guy..." gripes vied with whispered schemes to beat the rap.

Kids cried. Mother nursed. A schizophrenic acted out in one corner. A teenage couple necked in another. Once in a while an old black man would go up and down the line handing out cards saying he was a deaf mute and could we please help pay for his ear operation.

I remember the first time I came here, when it was finally my turn to go in and meet with an examiner. In spite of the doings in the hallway I had somehow visualized a courtroom setting on the other side of the examination room door. Or maybe a judge's old chambers with rich wood paneling and shelves of law books reaching up to the ceiling.

But the examiner's room turned out to be an old broom closet. There were still boxes of cleaning supplies piled up next to mops and brooms in one corner. The only other furnishings and ornaments were an American flag in a corner not occupied by cleaning items, a picture of President Reagan, a single wooden chair, and a small metal table.

On the table was a tape recorder, a large black ledger, a stack of those cards explaining the state law that made ticketing protests so hopeless, and an intercom that I assumed could be used to summon the female Vopo in the hallway by the elevator.

The room's only chair was occupied by the examiner. I had to stand. This was another hint (in case I hadn't caught on before) that this phony excuse for a hearing wouldn't take very long.

My examiner was a narrow-faced little guy with thinning blond hair and ears so oversized he could have bought them at Disneyland. I'd heard the city used third year Suffolk Law School students as examiners. If this guy was a law school senior he must have graduated college at twelve. He was writing something in the black ledger when I entered and didn't bother looking up for a minute or two. So I thought I'd break the ice.

"This is a broom closet," I said.

"Not any more," he replied.

He added a last note to his ledger entry, closed the book, favored me with a bored shitless look of utter disinterest. "My name is Morris," he said. "I've been authorized to hear your reason or reasons for contesting a parking ticket issued by a Boston parking agent. Did you bring the ticket with you?"

He held out his hand. I passed over the ticket

He then flipped on the tape recorder on the table, repeated his own name, the date and time, my ticket number, along with the offense (parking in a loading zone), the location of the loading zone, the time and place the ticket was issued, and the parking agent's name.

"Have you read your rights?" he asked. "They're listed on the card the guard gave you when you got off the elevator. If you feel you have to leave this room to read the card, you'll have to get at the end of the line."

He smiled at his own little joke. It was a weak smile, perhaps because he had already told this joke twenty times that day and would tell it another twenty or thirty times before they let him go back to the Suffolk law library later that afternoon.

I glanced down at the card. Its Item 4, which I knew by heart, was printed in red ink and read as follows:

"In accordance with Chapter 190 of the Acts of 1982 and Massachusetts General Law, Chapter 90, Section 20A1/2, a ticket affixed (attached) to a motor vehicle...shall be deemed sufficient notice, and a certificate (signature) of the officer affixing such notice that it has been affixed...[and] shall be

deemed prima facie evidence (enough to establish a fact
or infraction) and shall be admissible in any judicial or
administrative proceedings as the facts contained herein."

These words were highlighted in red ink because they spelled
out the game. Getting the ticket meant you deserved to get the
ticket.

"This is pure bullshit," I said, pointing at the card.

"Oh?" His finger dangled above the intercom switch. I
remembered the guard's sidearm. It was so big it should have
been wheel-mounted.

"But it doesn't matter. I have proof that the meter maid...."

"Parking agent."

"...proof the parking agent should never have issued the ticket."

"Proof?" The examiner's finger moved away from the switch.
"Proof that would allow me to nullify your fine is difficult to
produce in these cases. As you know from reading our little card.
Of course, if you really do have proof..."

He smiled again, adding a kind of raspy giggle. His long face,
those big ears, that awful giggle, suddenly unnerved me.

Maybe I'd misjudged my surroundings. Maybe I hadn't
stumbled into a bad remake of Hersey's *Petition For More
Space*. Maybe I hadn't even fallen down a Lewis Carroll rabbit
hole or entered a Kafkian castle. The Vopo outside and the
tape recorder in this tiny room had me thinking now of Arthur
Koestler's *Darkness At Noon*.

Nonetheless, I believed even the worst tyrants must bow before
straight-forward pictorial evidence when it's presented to them.

I reached into an envelope I'd been carrying and placed two photos on the table in front of the examiner.

"That first one shows my car parked where I got the ticket," I said confidently. "You can still see the ticket on the windshield. Notice the area to the right and above the car, where I've drawn an arrow. It's tree foliage. Then look at the second picture. It shows what's hidden behind that foliage. The sign saying I can't park there because it's a loading zone. But no one could possibly see that sign. At least not in summer, when the tree is blooming. So the meter maid..."

"Parking agent," he interrupted.

"...shouldn't have issued the ticket," I proclaimed.

The examiner stroked his narrow chin. "Not bad," he said after a few seconds.

"These are like those 8 X 10 shots taken by Officer Obey in *Alice's Restaurant*." I replied. "Let's hope this isn't another case of blind justice."

He giggled in response.

The peculiar horror of the fictional society in *My Petition For More Space* is that no matter how often you come back to petition, or how strong is your argument, you never win. The other side always outsmarts you. Your request is never granted.

But maybe, I was thinking, with respect to my own parking petition, I just might win. This parking ticket examiner was a student. A law student, true, but even so. And his giggled response to my last remark gave me hope that he might take the view that since we were both, down deep, cool Arlo Guthrie-loving dudes, I had a shot. My hopes soared.

"Now show me the other photo," he said after a few seconds.

"What other photo?"

"Well, I can see that this is your car because the first photo shows the license plate number that's on the parking ticket."

"Of course."

"And I can see that there's a ticket on the windshield of your car.

"Yes."

"And your ticketed car is clearly under a loading zone sign that's hidden by tree foliage.

"That's what I said."

"What I don't have is anything showing me that this hidden sign under which your car is parked in the picture is the same sign, on the same street, where this ticket was issued."

"Where else could it be?"

"Under a different loading zone sign that's obstructed by foliage in a different part of the city. You haven't proven that this is the actual hidden sign that caused you to be ticketed."

"You think I drove around Boston looking for a loading zone sign that was hidden by foliage so I could shoot fake photos that would get me out of paying a fifteen dollar parking fine?"

"Do I think that?" The examiner looked off into the distance as if to consider the matter seriously. "It certainly would require a great deal of effort to do such a thing. And the return on the effort would be relatively small...

He paused. "You know I'll be honest with you Mr..." He looked at a list of names in his black ledger, "Mr. Silverstein. Any relation to Edward Silverstein? He teaches at Suffolk."

I didn't know Edward Silverstein from a can of Maxwell House. "He's my uncle," I said.

"He almost failed me last year. Terrible teacher. A real bastard. But that's not your fault, is it.

"The thing is," he continued, "without proof that this is the same sign that caused your ticket to be issued, my hands are tied. Though I will tell you this: There's actually a pretty good chance that you did not, in fact, deserve this ticket.

"The pay window is on the third floor. Follow the crowd. I'm sure you'll find it."

He opened his big black ledger and began writing, his free hand hovering above the intercom switch all the while.

The local press is supposed to be the public's champion when to comes to exposing ripoffs emanating from City Hall. In Boston during the early 1980's it didn't work that way.

There were, of course, occasional stories in the daily papers about the most egregious outrages. You couldn't not run a piece about a handful of parking tickets being slipped under the windshield of a parked car whose front seat is occupied by a corpse.

The problem with the Boston Globe and the Boston Herald when it came to reporting about ticketing in these years was that the people who ran both papers saw themselves as members of the city's leadership cadre. Ferocious ticketing being part of the make-Boston-a-world-class-city credo, members of this mature and responsible political culture understood the necessity of sticking it to local motorists for the greater good.

Being not only immature and irresponsible myself, and worse, literate, I immediately thought the best gorilla action here was to write a book about local parking horrors. No publishing house anywhere, to the best of my knowledge, had ever published a book addressing parking ticket angst or was likely to be interested in the subject. So I did one with Kay.

These days that would present no problem for an author. You can use Amazon, Barnes & Noble and a few other platforms to inexpensively self-publish. In the 1980s, however, would-be self publishers tended to go the costly vanity press route and end up selling just a few copies to friends and relatives.

I was much luckier in this regard. I was dating and preparing to share a life with a wonderful artist and illustrator, Kay Wood. I also had a friend with after-hours access to a type setting word processor (a fairly unusual thing in those years). I had another long-time friend who was in charge of publications at a large consulting firm, and she allowed me to use her contacts with a printer to get my work published at a very modest cost.

Of greatest importance, I had a great subject and a great idea about how to package and peddle what even today may still be the most poignant book about parking ticketing even published in America, and perhaps the known universe—*The Little Book Of Boston Parking Horrors*.

Writing it proved amazingly easy. Kay and I simply approached twenty-five Boston people picked at random from among friends, neighbors and local merchants, and asked them if they had ever had a really nasty encounter with a local meter maid or any other minion of the Boston Parking Authority. From this extremely limited pool we came away with twenty usable horror stories. Of the five contacts with no terrible tale to tell, four had never driven a car in Boston, and one was dating a meter maid and thought she was doing a great job.

Numbers like these let me know, right from the get-go, that we were really on to something. And the stories themselves, though none featured a corpse, were perfectly indicative of the extreme lengths local authorities were going to get motorists' money.

People were being issued parking tickets during hurricanes and blizzards. Cars were being towed at two in the morning from in front of clubs that stayed opened until three. Meter maids were spotted hiding behind buildings, waiting to pounce if a motorist without change for a meter ran off to get some at a nearby store. People were being arrested for two or three overdue parking tickets. Whole neighborhoods were shunned by savvy drivers because of the reputations of the meter maids who operated there, in much the way that savvy Central Africans avoid lands where tsetse flies roam freely.

The book was fleshed out with a city map showing the most ticket-prone areas, a brief history of ticketing, a photo section, and a directory of phone numbers that might prove useful for victims of the parking system. Kay did some hysterically funny illustrations for the book, including a real grabber on the cover that depicted a cop writing out a ticket while a woman is being strangled nearby and another woman is running away from a guy with a hatchet. The overall effect was heightened by the cover stock we used. It was the same garish orange color as a parking ticket.

When the book was typeset and printed, the gorilla was ready to roll.

You couldn't sell self-published books online in the mid-1980's because there was no online worth mentioning. Al Gore had yet to finish inventing the Internet. Fortunately, I had an even better way to peddle a Boston parking horrors book with a local focus and a waiting readership.

There were then about three dozen bookstores in the Greater Boston area. Some were part of chains. Some were independents. But all in those days gave their managers and assistant managers considerable discretion in dealing with local publishers.

A manager or assistant manager could accept a small number of books, display them, and most importantly from my perspective, pay with cash from the register immediately after these books were sold. The ordering strings were far looser than they were soon to become, and a one-book publisher like myself didn't have to wait ninety, one hundred and twenty, or one hundred and fifty days for relatively meager payments.

The biggest things I had going for me in marketing terms, however, were not just my book's subject and its very modest $5.95 cover price, but the assistant managers at most Boston-Cambridge book stores.

I had dated a few women like these before Kay came along. Most seemed to be in their late twenties or early thirties, chubby, between relationships, with wonderful bedroom eyes behind thick glasses. They drove eight-year-old Volkswagens with holes in the floorboards and exteriors decorated with floral paste-ons. They lived on the top floors of as-yet-ungentrified triple deckers in Somerville, in rooms with purple walls and old college text books, paperbacks, and L.P.s piled floor to ceiling. Places that smelled of cat shit, broccoli, marijuana, and maybe a little of recent male visitors.

These women didn't work in bookstores to gain experience in retail management. They worked in bookstores because they loved books. It was a love that strongly inclined them to like writers. Genuinely like writers. Even respect writers. Think the work of writers might actually have intrinsic value.

No, *The Little Book Of Boston Parking Horrors* wasn't *Leaves Of Grass*. But Walt Whitman had peddled his own books store to store, sometimes door to door, and these women had not only read Whitman, they appreciated a writer who wasn't too good to peddle the same way.

A guy like me would come into their store, dressed like a ragpicker, tall, hunched, bearded, twitching with nervous energy, a dozen of my own books under one arm, walk up to the front counter where this assistant manager was usually standing and say:

"Gotten any parking tickets lately?"

The line never failed to get a response like: "I've been waiting all day for someone to ask me that."

Then she would tell me her own tale of ticketing woe. After which she'd break into laughter accompanied by cries of "Yes! Yes! Yes!" upon examining Kay's cover and inside illustrations, and order at least a dozen copies of our book. These invariably got placed right next to the cash register where customers couldn't fail to see them when checking out a purchase.

Every Friday I would make the rounds of 'my' stores, schmooze the assistant managers, share stories about the newest ticketing abominations, do a little business. I would restock the books that had sold that week. The managers would tap the register and give me my sixty percent of the book's cover price.

This wasn't a lot of money per book. But each store seemed to sell most of the stock I'd left behind every week, and there were three dozen stores. Very soon I was sold out of the first printing of 2,500 copies, and people all over Boston were waving copies of *The Little Book Of Boston Horrors* at meter maids the way students during the Cultural Revolution in China waved Mao's *Little Red Book* at enemies in Mao's version of a communist state.

What do people really care about?

Like many folks who have been burdened down by an overly generous education I got this one wrong for many years. I thought the state of the economy, ecological well-being, world peace, these were the things that deeply concerned my fellow Americans. Or maybe sex, drugs and rock and roll. It wasn't until the early 1980's, while living in Boston, that I learned the real answer to this question — a place to park their cars without getting clipped in the process.

Thus it was that with the publication of *The Little Book Of Boston Parking Horrors* I had finally tapped into this mother load of human longing and became an instant celebrity.

Patrons at the Dunkin' Donuts in J.P. raised their coffee mugs when I came in for my morning brew. I was lovingly tapped on the shoulder by taxi drivers and truckers as I walked down the street. A local restaurant named one of its humus dishes after the book that Kay and I had produced. My barber kissed my bald spot when I came in for a trim. I had become The People's Defender.

Kay and I were even honored guests at a champagne reception held at a Charles Street art gallery, whose owner had very good reasons to dislike the meter maids who were scaring off his big spending customers. When it came to ticketing, Boston had finally achieved a kind of social equality— equality of abuse at the hands of public officialdom. Blue-haired ladies at this reception gave us the same thumbs up that Kay and I were getting in coffee shops and on the streets from people of other social classes.

Stories about the book (and from the book) appeared in newspapers, along with sidebars suggesting that the local press was finally feeling pressure to report on the extent of local parking ticket predation. I did radio, of course, and some television as well.

One such tube appearance was especially memorable because it brought me into contact with a man who might have actually turned my ticketing crusade into some real policy changes. A man, alas, who was destined to seek public office with one of history's worst political slogans.

His name was David Finnegan. He was a local Boston pol running for mayor against a long-time, unpopular incumbent, Kevin White. Finnegan's TV show was a vehicle to promote his candidacy. I was a guest on the show because its host understood that parking tickets were a very nasty form of taxation, and therefore had a lot of populist potential as a political issue.

Finnegan had a good shot at the job. He was handsome. He was Irish. He was articulate. He had his own TV show. Then he unveiled his campaign slogan. It was meant to encapsulate the fact that the present mayor had been too long in office: "Him again or Finnegan," ran the slogan.

No one who lived in Boston at the time will ever forget this slogan—though heaven knows we've all tried. His campaign went down in flames, a victim of bad verse. With it went my only real hope of putting a lid on Boston curb tax abuse.

There's no happy ending to this gorilla effort in Boston. The election I was hoping to influence in that town came and went, and the tickets kept coming at the same or increased levels. The sad truth is that if local officials can simply sweat out a couple of years of public fury, very aggressive parking ticketing becomes just another unpleasant but accepted element of urban life.

It wasn't until I moved to Philadelphia that I had one clear victory as a ticket-fighting gorilla. Kay and I published a local edition of our Boston classic, titling it *The Little Book Of Philadelphia Parking Horrors.* It was structured much like the Boston edition but didn't sell nearly as well. Folks in Philly had already become too accepting of the ticketing lash, regarding it as just another local horror to be sullenly endured like watching the local professional football team fail to win a Super Bowl for decades.

Then one day...

It was Easter Sunday, 1994, an absolutely perfect spring day. Bright, cloudless, mid-70's, low humidity. Kay and I, along with half the local population, including a very large number of families fresh from church, decided to take advantage of the weather and stroll in Philadelphia's Fairmount Park, one of the natural treasures designed by Frederick Law Olmstead in the late nineteenth century, and by far the largest urban park in the United States.

To get to a walking area in the park people had to drive down a long leafy road called Kitchen Lane and park in a small dirt lot next to the start of a walking trail. We parked, took a lovely walk, and when we returned to our car an hour later found a ticket on the windshield — a ticket like the one on every other car in the area. The local constabulary had used the cover of Easter Sunday to give a big boost to its monthly ticket quota.

I wasn't so much angry as aghast. This had to be some kind of administrative error. But when I called the local parking authority the next day, and managed to get through to someone in the public affairs department, I was quickly disabused of this notion.

"How could you use Easter Sunday as an excuse to issue parking tickets to people taking a holiday stroll?" I asked.

"Easter Sunday?" the woman on the other end of line replied innocently. "We weren't ticketing Easter Sunday people. We were out ticketing in force because it was the first day of the fishing season."

No. This could not be allowed to stand. There had to be a bottom—even for a municipal parking authority.

I called a columnist at the Philadelphia Inquirer who I'd gotten to know by virtue of our parking horrors book, filled him in on the details, and he promised to give it some play. His story appeared a day or two later. Amid a great deal of local snickering, and for all I know a call from the Vatican, the Philadelphia Parking Authority backed down and rescinded every ticket given out anywhere in the city that Easter Sunday.

Chalk one up for the gorilla. Final score in my long battle against the curb taxers: Taxers 99, gorilla 1.

At least it wasn't a total shut out.

IV.
Changed Perspectives:
A Gorilla In Europe On Sam's Dime

After escaping the fevered but shallow waters of late 1940s and early 1950s Bensonhurst Brooklyn, but before taking up gorilla arms in defense of the great Star Sol, I had a number of other experiences and encounters that shaped my approach to life in various ways. I was a social worker. I was a Jewish military policeman in Nuremberg, Germany. I met my wife-to-be in Munich while keeping another woman in Paris.

About the social work. I've never really cared all that much about poor people's economic well-being. Not viscerally anyway. It was just that intellectually it struck me as kind of dumb that in a country as rich as the United States was in the 1950s and 1960s, there should be so many people who were still so poor.

In the early 1960s I was thus prepped to sign up for what was America's last great war. Maybe the most noble war ever undertaken by this country. Maybe even in the whole world. The War on Poverty that was declared by President Lyndon Johnson in his 1964 State of the Union address.

It wasn't that easy to enlist, however. The obvious way was to get a job with New York City's Department of Welfare. The problem was that there were so many other people who thought it was worthwhile to fight this war, and only a limited number of slots for new social workers, that the competition was intense.

To even apply you had to show up at a Manhattan armory, the only place big enough to accommodate all the applicants. There you had to wait on long lines to fill out paperwork and explain to an interviewer why you deserved to help the poor.

While waiting my own turn on one of these lines I saw an amazing sight. A young guy was carried into the armory on a stretcher by some friends and took his place in line, on the floor, horizontally, pulled toward an interviewer by one of his carriers so as not to miss the opportunity to help alleviate poverty.

His reasoning for doing all this, I'm certain, was that he believed what we all believed in those days. That when in the future our grandchildren asked: "What was poverty, granddad," we would be able to describe this long gone phenomenon accurately from first hand observations.

That morning in the armory. Those long lines. The guy carried in on a stretcher so he wouldn't miss the chance to help eliminate poverty. I love this country. But nothing else before or since has ever made me so proud to be an American.

Anyway. I got the job and became a not all that caring social worker. While there I met another social worker who really did care. More amazingly, she came to care about me, too.

This was not an easy thing to do at the time. I was fairly good looking and well spoken for someone who had never escaped Brooklyn (the old Brooklyn, that is, not its present incarnation as the hippest place on the Eastern seaboard). But even after attending Brooklyn grade and high schools, I just took a short bus ride to attend Brooklyn College.

The resulting me was thus an unpolished neighborhood kid, inexperienced, unsophisticated, insecure in every way possible. Fortunately my first real lover, Betsy D., shared something with me that miraculously overcame all these shortcomings. We were both really, really horny and committed to doing everything possible to alleviate the condition.

Very soon we were living together in an area where this was the norm. We got a ratty apartment on Avenue D in Manhattan, in the old Lower East Side slum that had morphed into the new East Village, a multi-racial, artsy bohemia swimming in marijuana fumes. A neighborhood where you could get stoned just breathing on a walk to a local bodega.

During working hours I was giving out money to poor people. Late at night and on weekends I was getting stoned and doing my best to make up for a long teenage sexual drought. To help fill some of the leftover times I decided to get a master's degree at the Brazilian Institute of New York University, one of just two places in this country back then where studies of Brazil were being undertaken seriously.

For reasons I can no longer remember and which probably didn't even make sense at the time, I chose as the subject for my master's thesis the Brazilian military in the nineteenth century. Then a reason appeared that seemed to make this oddball choice of subject prescient. I got my Greetings.

For those old enough to remember when this country still had a military draft, the word 'Greetings' has a special meaning. It was the word that topped a notice from your local draft board ordering you to appear at the nearest induction center where you would be examined to see if you qualified for service in the U.S. Army.

A great many young Americans in the 1960s, upon getting their Greetings in the mail, took evasive action to avoid serving. I

didn't. Where I grew up, when you were called, you served. It
seemed like an obvious adjunct to being part of a democratic
society in which rich and poor from all sections and strata of
society came together for an equal share of abuse or worse.

There was also the fact that I was one of this country's foremost
experts about Brazil's nineteenth century military. In fact, almost
certainly The foremost expert because no one else cared enough
about the subject to bother, and I'd heard that the U.S. Army
had a small presence of some kind in Rio de Janeiro. I figured
that with my specialized background Rio was certain to be my
posting, and I could spend my military service improving my
samba skills, studying Carnival rituals at close range, and maybe
writing a monograph about nude bathing on Copa Cabana beach.

As long tradition dictated, I got good and drunk the night
before going to the Whitehall Street induction center in Lower
Manhattan for my personal meeting with military destiny.
Enclosed with every Greetings was carfare to the center where
they had your physical. This being New York City, the carfare
was a subway token. Just one. You weren't expected to need
return fare.

The Whitehall Street induction center wasn't quite as surreal as
Arlo Guthrie made it out to be in his classic "Alice's Restaurant"
anti-war cry from the heart. But it was nutty enough. And
revealing. Anyone who still believed that humans are made
in the image of God quickly lost that article of faith with one
look at the line of naked and hung over American males, circa
1964, stumbling along to have all their orifices (yes, all of them)
examined.

My own close encounter with failure in this induction ritual
came during the final test before we were to be sworn in. The
test for diabetes.

We were led into a very large room with toughs along its walls and piped in sounds of running water. A set up designed to inspire urination. Each of us was given a metal cup and told to fill it.

One by one this instruction was followed until there remained only two non-pee-ers, me and another inductee. "You don't do it, we use a catheter," announced a cup collecting sergeant, who then left the room, leaving the other guy and me to contemplate this frightening possibility.

Another minute or two went by and this other guy did what had to be done. I still hadn't. We looked at each other. I asked the obvious question. "Can I borrow half?"

He shrugged. "Enjoy," he said, pouring me a generous measure.

My admission into military service was thus celebrated with half a tin cup of borrowed piss.

Basic training lasted eight weeks. At its close I learned my MOS — Military Occupational Specialty. It wasn't in intelligence or anything else likely to get me to that dream posting in Rio de Janeiro. They made me a military policeman instead.

Why? O.K. I was 6'3", weighed about 190 pounds, I could drive a double shift army jeep. I guess this, along with a college education that would enable me to write up arrest reports, were the key qualifications.

Or not. Go figure. It was the army. I felt lucky they didn't make me a cook.

From basic training I went off to MP specialty training in Fort Gordon in Augusta, Georgia where I had a curious and in a way inspiring lesson in ethnicity. I was lying in my bunk one evening before bed check and Murphy came over.

Murphy looked like a Murphy. Red haired, thickset, pug nosed. He stood next to my bunk, leaned over, and started talking to me in Yiddish.

My folks sometime spoke Yiddish at home, so while I was never interested enough to learn the language, I knew it when I heard it. I asked the obvious question (I always seemed to be asking obvious questions): "How come you speak Yiddish, Murphy?"

The reason, it turned out, was because his family lived in Boston and his father was the only non-Jew in that city's bagel baking union. After working all day with Yiddish speakers he would speak it at home and his kids learned it, too.

When we later got our duty assignments, both Murphy and I were sent to Germany. Where presumably the locals could puzzle over why an American named Murphy could speak Yiddish and one named Silverstein couldn't.

In Germany I was stationed in Nuremberg, the brownest town in the country before and during WWII. Being a Jewish cop there, even twenty year's after war's end, was an interesting experience in a number of ways.

Some of the strangest things I encountered in the year-and-a-half I served there, however, were the product of American army policies insensitive to the point of total idiocy. Like the location the army chose for its centralized laundry facility, which serviced American troops in a broad geographic area. They sited it on the grounds of the old Dachau concentration camp.

When it was my turn to take my unit's sheets and pillowcases for cleaning, I loaded up a jeep and drove to Dachau, about 80 miles from Nuremberg. Turning off a small road I came to a pleasant street with attractive and well tended housing on both sides, where camp guards and their families once lived, and where some U.S. Army personnel lived now. At the end of this street, making another turn, I came to the old camp itself, unchanged from war days, a large number of incredibly ugly ramshackle structures still encircled by barbed wire with guard towers at regular intervals.

From the main gate of the camp a stone walkway led in the direction of a squat two-story concrete building. Its first and second floors were probably used for camp administration, also the American army's present use. This walkway itself, however, led to a short set of stairs that took you down to the building's basement.

It didn't take much imagination or special insight to recognize that this stairway to a basement area, fronted by a thick wooden door, was where enhanced mistreatment had once been meted out to camp prisoners. One entered here now to drop off sheets and pillow cases.

Inside was a long counter where laundry was spread out so it could be counted and tagged by a friendly corporal who gave you a receipt. He then sent you off with a cheery, southern accented: "Hurry on back to Dachau, hear."

On the main gate of the camp once hung the infamous 'Arbeit macht frei 'sign. Here, a few steps away, was an American army laundry specialist telling you to hurry back.

Just an enlisted man's attempt at black humor? Certainly. But
here not the sort of sendoff easily forgotten. It was something
that let you know, in case you didn't know it before, that even
the largest entities, military and civilian, public and private, are
capable of huge institutional stupidity.

I didn't get shipped to Viet Nam, but it was close. A lot of troops
originally stationed in Germany got sent there when things
heated up in a big way. I was lucky enough to get my honorable
discharge in Europe and begin my own bum around there before
that became very common.

Betsy quit social work in New York and joined me. We set up
light housekeeping in Munich's hip Schwabing District. I got a
job working as a civilian for the army in Wurtzburg, a few miles
up the road from Munich. The money was very good. I was
paid in U.S. dollars trading one-for-four-German-marks in those
years.

After a few months living together in Munich, Betsy told me
she had always dreamed of living in Paris. I had lots of money
coming in. So…what the heck.

She went off to Paris and I helped support her there. I still had
plenty left over to live comfortably in Munich.

While Betsy was away in the City Of Lights I met Suzanne,
the woman who was to become my wife. She was intelligent,

attractive and adventuresome. She spoke excellent German and was much better able to fully mix in with the Munich demimonde than was I.

We made an attractive couple. Shared that era's taste in pleasures and politics. But in almost all the really basic elements necessary to maintain a long and successful relationship we didn't make much sense.

We were, in other words, a prototypical 1960s destined-to-fail pairing. The kind of mistake almost everyone immersed in that decade's ethos was likely to make, and indeed, probably should have made as part of a life worth looking back on with a wistful and forgiving adult smile.

Not surprisingly, Betsy was not happy when she returned from Paris and learned I was about to run off with another woman. As part of her recompense for my unfaithfulness she took an unkind (but admittedly deserved) revenge.

Inheriting our Munich apartment she got the use of its phone, which was under my name. In the weeks after I left town but before the line was disconnected she invited every foreigner she could find to come and use it to call home. The U.S., Australia, Thailand, Outer Mongolia, wherever.

I don't know exactly how big a phone bill was run up. I suspect, though, that what with penalties and interest added on, the total owed now probably approximates the current national debt of Greece.

Hell hath no fury...

V.
Environmental Follies
(The Gorilla Bonds With Mother Gaia)

There's always been a strange affinity between my gorilla activities and real estate. Being offered property, inheriting property, selling property on unbelievably favorable terms, occupying property rent- or mortgage-free because of an even more unbelievable set of circumstances, are things that have underwritten a number of my gorilla efforts. A property deal was thus to become a major supporter of my work on behalf of Mother Gaia, a lady I served longer and even more faithfully than old Father Sol.

My labors as a gaian gorilla began a decade-and-a-half after being granted a solar vision in Miami with the help of Ft. Pierce property peddlers, and shortly after I abandoned my crusade against Boston's ticketing ghouls. I was visiting Miami again — or more exactly, North Miami Beach — on another property-related mission.

North Miami Beach in the 1980s was a kind of elephant burial grounds for elderly New York City Jews. Sensing the end was near they instinctively flocked here to expire. Their last years were then spent racing from air-conditioned cars to air-conditioned hotel lobbies and restaurants, opening bank accounts to get the Tupperware given new depositors, receiving treatments at geriatric health clinics, lobbying for Israel, and rifling the condo units of their recently deceased peers for valuables before the deceased's children arrived and got all the good stuff.

When my mom died and my sister and I came down to settle her estate, we found her small living quarters had been pretty thoroughly tossed. My father had died a few years earlier and some of his three-button suits were still in the closet, presumably because the building's in-house hunter-gatherers didn't like the style or fit. Some appliances and heavy furniture had also not been carted away. Other clothes, however, along with my mom's jewelry, small house wares, and the family's splendid collection of classic Mickey Katz albums, had all been methodically picked over.

One of the building's elderly tenants came by while my sister and I were cleaning up the mess and doing an inventory. He was a man of about seventy wearing tan shorts that exposed his knock knees, and a flowered short-sleeved shirt open down the front to reveal a regal growth of gray-white chest hair. He came through the apartment's front door without knocking and seemed both surprised and annoyed to find us there.

"You must be the children," he sniffed, looking us up and down with the practiced eye of someone who has seen this undeserving ilk many times before. "Don't forget to leave the air-conditioner on when you leave," he said, "or the mold will spread to other units."

A real estate agent who came by later in the day told us we had two choices when it came to mom's condo unit. We could sell it, or we could keep it to use as a vacation home. "This is really a great place to vacation," he added.

Rather than spend our future winter vacations with our souvenir-hunting visitor and his mates we opted to sell. My share of the sale price provided me with a bit of capital to go with my newly acquired Tupperware collection.

Solvency has always made me nervous. So when my modest inheritance cleared probate and the North Miami Beach condo sale was finalized, I quit a job I didn't like, began spending a lot of time with my son Jon, wrapped up my forlorn attempts to save Boston motorists from ticketing ghouls, and commenced doing some serious research in a field then out of favor but which I found strangely fascinating — the environment.

Not surprisingly, my inheritance soon withered away. My one remaining asset was another condo—one I'd bought in the Jamaica Plain section of Boston when I first got back from settling family financial matters in Florida. And what a purchase this J.P. homestead turned out to be!

I had moved into this dwelling when it was still a rental apartment and lived there as a tenant. The building was a gem. Its units had not been divided and divided again to accommodate gaggles of students as was the case with most similar Boston properties. My seven room apartment was spacious, well laid out, had a working fireplace, and a claw foot bath tub.

Such features made the building containing my rental unit an obvious candidate for condo conversion in Boston's then rapidly gentrifying housing market. The problem for a would-be gentrifier was that the building was in Jamaica Plain, a neighborhood with strong populist inclinations and a feisty, combative collection of community groups. Like the underground coal fires in Centralia, Pennsylvania that neither human effort nor prayer seemed able to extinguish, out-of-vogue notions like affordable housing and a fair shake for the non-rich had somehow not been smoldered out of existence in Jamaica Plain. Building owners who heedlessly rushed to convert attractive rental apartments into condominiums got whacked here by endless legal challenges and community protests for their efforts.

The owner of the building where I was living therefore decided to take a more tenant-friendly approach. He made the offering price to current occupants like myself a very modest forty-two thousand dollars, and any tenant who could come up with a twenty percent down payment of eight thousand and change could buy his or her unit. Even tenants with past credit problems would not be disqualified because the landlord agreed to guarantee their mortgages.

It was the perfect made-for-me deal. I had the worst credit rating on the East Coast. My role model when it came to servicing bank debt was my Uncle Sid, who is credited with inventing serial bankruptcy in the nineteen-thirties and turning it into a recognized American lifestyle option. With cash from my recent North Miami Beach property sale, for the first time in my life I had eight thousand dollars in loose capital. I bought in.

Two years after this Boston purchase, to the surprise of no one who knew me then or since, I was once again broke. So broke, in fact, that I had fallen several months behind in my condo fees and was being threatened with a takeover action by the condo association. It was then that the gods of real estate intervened.

Kay and I were coming down the stairs of my third floor unit one Saturday morning and came upon a guy I didn't know loitering in the building's front hallway.

"Can I help," I asked?

"Yeah. I'm trying to find the bell for 2B."

"That's the unit directly under mine. Are you a friend?"

"No. Actually I'm a potential unit buyer."

"I didn't know it was for sale. Mind if I ask how much she's asking?"

"A hundred and fifty. But I'm pretty sure I can knock her down." The visitor gave me a wink.

I almost fainted. A hundred and fifty thousand dollars? I had bought the same size unit and layout for forty-two just a couple of years earlier. I'd heard Boston was experiencing a real estate boom but this was madness. That same afternoon I listed my own property for sale with a J.P. broker and gave her a set of keys.

The following Saturday morning Kay and I went out for a walk around Boston Common. I told my new real estate agent we'd be back in a few hours. When we did get back there was a note on the kitchen table saying that I had a "firm offer for $140,000." It turned out to be a very solid offer because the guy who made it had just sold a place of his own for two hundred and twenty thousand dollars and was able to buy my place for cash.

I ended up clearing about a hundred thousand dollars in two years on a cash investment of eight thousand dollars after listing the property for a single week. Not bad. Though I was destined, in a very curious and backhanded way, to do even better on a real estate transaction a few years later.

Most of this J.P. condo money was earmarked for Jon's education and for a down payment on a new house I would buy with Kay in Philadelphia. As for the remainder, well, it could go into solid investments or it could be used to underwrite my next gorilla adventure. Character being destiny, I opted for the latter, though not without a sense of foreboding.

The first time I'd heeded the call of the gorilla in the 1970s it was a rush. I couldn't wait to wade into the fray. When the call to gorilla action on parking tickets came a few years later it was still an amusing enough prospect to get my juices flowing. By the time I was called to try and save the environment in the late 1980s and early 1990s, however, I didn't want to answer the phone. I knew the routine by now. I knew where things were headed. I knew my always tenuous hold on a middle class lifestyle would soon experience another bout of gorilla interruptus.

Playing Cyrano de Bergerac is a young man's sport. Beyond a certain age, an appealing and energetic rebel can all too easily come across like an angry and embittered crank. By the time I attempted to save nature from the misguided and highly destructive ministrations of people who purported to be environmental protectors I was almost fifty. I needed a 401(k), not another stint on the front lines of gorilladom. Signs were already abundant that my physical and mental abilities were beginning to correlate with my calendar age. Indeed, I distinctly remember the night I began to suspect I might actually be getting old.

It happened just about the time I sold the J.P. condo, while I still pretty much fancied myself a beamish boy. Kay and I were at an Elvis Costello concert in the Cape Cod Coliseum. The place was packed and noisy, aglow and crackling with audience energy. A dirt floor space in front of the stage had been left free of chairs so people could dance there during an intermission.

Pogo dancing was popular at the time. Pogo is a kind of slam dance where participants bounce up and down like they're on pogo sticks. Guys bounced around each other and off each other (it was pretty much a guy's thing), the moves dependent on an individual's balance and how much beer he'd consumed before arriving at the dance floor.

It looked like fun. So I wended my way to the dance area and commenced my own version of this manly exercise.

In the midst of scores of jostling male bodies, one of my swinging elbows caught another Pogo dancer on the side of the head. He was a young guy. Taller than me and a lot heavier built. He had several tattoos, an earring, a shaved scalp. The instant my elbow connected he stopped bouncing and cocked his arm.

Then he saw who hit him. Looked puzzled. Dropped his fist and apologized. "Sorry," he said, and off he bounced.

Sorry? I didn't want to get decked, of course, but an apology? With not even a "fuck you" thrown in? I was shattered.

There are worse pains than getting cold-cocked by a shave-headed bozo on a Pogo dance floor. Like the painful realization that said bozo thinks knocking you on your ass would be as devoid of macho meaning as knocking down his elderly Uncle Irwin. I slunk back to my seat, feeling a sudden, desperate urge to down a fifth of Geritol.

Maybe that's when I should have retired from the gorilla game. But no. Father Sol had needed my help before. Mother Gaia called out to me now. And no matter the odds or the inconvenience, when the chips are down, a gorilla's gotta do what a gorilla's gotta do.

Halfway through Ronald Reagan's second term as President,
the environment as a political issue looked to be dead as a
doorknob. This was largely due to notions about the relationship
between environmental well-being and economic well-being
that pervaded virtually every environmental debate. Everyone
seemed to agree that we could either enjoy clean air and pure
water and protect nature, or we could enjoy continued economic
growth and material prosperity. But we couldn't have it both
ways.

Environmental groups bought into this thinking and opted to
support nature, even if it meant the loss of jobs and profits.
Business groups and most economists bought into this same
thinking, but opted for jobs and profits over nature.

Because Reagan and company fronted for industries that were
responsible for much of the country's (and indeed the world's)
pollution, promoting environmental protection was not part of
his administration's agenda, Nor, for that matter, was it at the
top of most Americans' personal agendas in the mid-1980s, as
economic insecurity superseded environmental enthusiasm.

A long history of a certain kind of environment-and-economy
thinking kept even very bright people from seeing new realities
in these years. This relationship goes back a long way.

Great lords were the most energetic protectors of nature against
the predations of peasants during the centuries of European
feudalism. For purely selfish reasons these lordly landowners
wanted streams and forests preserved *au naturale* so as to be

more entertaining places to conduct their outings. Peasants in this same period wanted a few extra scraps for the table and a bit more tillage. If that meant deforesting and poaching other species to extinctions, well, they had more immediate concerns.

As the Industrial Revolution took hold, an environment-over-economy counter culture came into being. It brought together old wealth with artsy romantics and a leftist intellectual elite. Its chief opposition, meanwhile, had a more democratic and populist tinge, reflecting its peasant-poacher-entrepreneurial antecedents. Mining, manufacturing, and other heavily polluting economic activities were then not only providing a growing number of jobs for poor people who desperately needed work, they were giving a fair number of people on the lower rungs of the social and economic ladder a means to rise higher.

Such was the basic environment-economic conflict at the start of the twentieth century—though in the real world, of course, this simple two-sided model was anything but simple, and was to become less and less simple as the century progressed. Within some highly successful families, one generation of rapaciously polluting money-makers gave birth to new generations of nature protecting environmentalists. Becoming generous contributors to environmental causes joined gifting cultural, educational, and medical institutions as a highly acceptable way to launder new money.

As more people in the richest countries became personally richer and middle class, environmental protection in developed countries was increasingly viewed as a necessary element of their good life. For countless middle managers and professionals this seemed to create conflicts of interests and even conflicts of conscience because they still believed goals of prosperity and environmental well-being were difficult if not impossible to reconcile.

By the latter decades of the twentieth century, however, there was really no need for such conflicts. The real problem was intellectual inertia.

After the 1960s it should have been clear to everyone that countries with the most stringent and best enforced environmental laws—the United States, Japan and nations of Western Europe—were the most prosperous, while countries with the worst environmental records—notably in the old Soviet Bloc—were piss poor and falling further behind year by painful year. Socialism, in fact, at least insofar as that system was practiced in the Soviet Union and its Eastern European clones, was in the process of disintegrating, in large measure *because* of its abysmal environmental practices.

By the mid-1980s I'd been writing about business off and on for years (when not gorilla writing about alternative energy and parking tickets), and was in touch with environmental as well as business issues by virtue of my work with solar. I therefore found it astounding that the environmental debate still revolved around choosing between the environment and the economy. I decided to do something about it. Gorillawise.

With the sure and certain knowledge that this caper was not likely to turn out any better than my past gorilla efforts, I proceeded to invent a new environmental economics. And this time around, a gorilla game that I now found quite familiar would be played out on a far bigger stage.

Things started in the usual way. I'd been doing some freelance writing for a publication called Silvia Porter's Money Magazine.

It was early 1988 and I was sitting in the magazine's New York office with its editor, Pat Estess, discussing possible articles for a future issue.

"How about something related to the coming November elections," I suggested.

"I like," she replied. "Good tie-in. But where's the investment angle? How could a small investor buy particular stocks based on an election-related story?"

That's how we started discussing industries that might benefit big if another Republican replaced two-term outgoing President Reagan in the Oval Office, or if a Democrat took his place. In the midst of this discussion I had one of my brainstorms—this one doubtless the product of my recent environmental research. Since these brainstorms invariably boded personal trouble for me, you'd think I'd quickly move on to a new subject, or at least keep quiet until I'd had time to sleep it off. Alas, my mouth is wired to my brain. When the latter flashes, the former flaps instantaneously.

"Well," I said, "there's environmental cleanup."

"Environmental cleanup is an overhead expense," said Pat. "Where's the investment angle?"

"It's not just an overhead expense." And I began fleshing out the brainstorm.

Long before the nature-hating Reagan crew came into office, the public had been bombarded with the apparently unassailable truism that cleaning the environment was a huge cost that polluting industries could not afford without raising prices, losing profits, or cutting jobs. I saw things a bit differently.

Yes, environmental cleanup was a cost to polluters. But this money didn't disappear from the economy. It didn't go up in smoke. It went to companies that cleaned up the mess that polluting companies were creating. To put this another way, it was a huge wealth transfer from bad guys to good guys. Lost jobs and profits for polluters meant new jobs and more profits for polluter-cleaner-uppers.

This was step one in a new intellectual construct that I seemed to understand all at once and in its entirety. Since no company in its right mind would pay hefty pollution clean up costs forever, there would be huge incentives to change the way they did business so as not to pollute and bear these costs in the future. This effort would inevitably spur innovation and hasten modernization, which in turn would make these companies (and the countries where they operated) more competitive. Throw in the added marketing cache that companies acquire when they are perceived to be greener, and the reduced long-term cleanup liabilities that make their stock more attractive to analysts, and I pretty much had a complete new environmental economics to replace the outmoded model that had held sway for decades, if not centuries.

The article I did for Pat Estess was a survey piece that mentioned environmental companies as just one investment sector among many that might be significantly affected by the upcoming elections. But Pat's positive reaction to my insights hinted that I was on to something. And indeed I was.

Over the next few years, spanning the presidency of George Bush the Elder and the first term of Bill Clinton, scores of my articles, Op Ed pieces, columns and essays would appear in newspapers like The Wall Street Journal and New York Times, in industry publications like Chemical Week, in scholarly publications like Business and Society Review, and in accounting journals like CFO and Environmental Finance. I would write books on my new environmental economics for Longman, St. Martin's, and other houses; turn up on CNN,

FNN, CNBC and the ABC Evening News; write columns
for a number of magazines; and do regular environmental
commentaries on National Public Radio. I would also help create
an environmental business program at New York University
where for a time I became an adjunct professor, and speak at
institutions including Yale and the University of Pennsylvania.
I even became an advisor to Al Gore's 1992 vice-presidential
effort.

It as quite a ride for a guy with no educational credentials in
environmental studies or economics. And this time around I
would not back away from the scene of the crime just because
what I hoped would happen didn't happen and I had proven
myself gorilla worthy. I stuck around long enough to personally
experience the full measure of Establishment hypocrisy,
stupidity, and yes, vindictiveness.

My biggest ever self-publishing success in monetary terms (even
bigger than *The Little Book Of Boston Parking Horrors*) came
about because Establishment publishers in early 1988 were still
as backward in their thinking when it came to environmental
economics as the main combatants in this field. By this time
the world was coming out of its Reagan-induced environmental
torpor and reawakening to the dangers of unchecked polluting.
This reawakening was the underlying theme of a great many
news stories then starting to appear. This didn't seem to matter,
however, when I first tried to pitch a book proposal based on my
own fast-growing body of published articles and other media
appearances.

All I got from this proposal peddling were a lot of pats on the head. My reception from editors usually went something like this:

"I have a totally new way of looking at environmental clean up and its relationship to the economy," I would say.

"I was in Central Park during the first Earth Day in 1968," the editor would reply. "Wonderful times." The editor's smile would be warm and friendly. "I want you to know I personally support your cause."

"I don't have a cause," I would say. "I have a better way to run an economy."

"Those Reagan people have been awful," the editor would continue, at which point he or she would lean further across the desk as a sign of solidarity. "If it were up to me we'd publish nothing but books that told the truth about polluters and the need to simplify our lifestyles to save nature."

"I don't give a shit about nature. I grew up in Brooklyn," I would say. "And who wants a simpler lifestyle? There's a lot of money to be made from environmental cleanup and all the efficiencies to be realized from innovations that reduce pollution while they enhance efficiency."

"The people who run this place are very down on environmental books," the editor would confide, looking a little embarrassed.

By then I was invariably frantic. "I'm not proposing an environmental book. It's a business book. Business. Money. Profits. Book sales."

"Thank you for still caring," the editor would conclude with genuine affection, easing me out the door as gently as possible. "I wish there were more people like you who still really cared about the environment."

It was like whacking a pinata with a feather boa. No matter how hard I swung, no matter how many times or from what angle, the same recorded announcements came back. The imprinting here went very, very deep.

I strongly suspected (correctly as it turned out) that in a short while the reception to proposals like mine would change dramatically because impossible-to-ignore realities were in the process of changing. But I wasn't inclined to wait for this to happen.

Instead I wrote a book and published it myself. It was titled *The Environmental Industry Yearbook And Investment Guide.* Its first fifty pages were a monograph that outlined my new environmental economics. The remaining hundred pages consisted of two-page descriptions, along with financial data, of the country's fifty largest publicly traded environmental cleanup firms. This soft cover publication was printed and spiral bound at a local copy center and ready for sale in 1989.

The timing couldn't gave been better. That summer turned out to be unusually hot in many parts of the United States, and after eight years of hands-off environmental enforcement by the Reagan Administration pollution levels in many cities had risen sharply. Searing heat combined with pollution-linked breathing problems got the public very nervous. Then red bag hospital waste started washing up on beaches near New York City. There were reports of fish dying mysteriously in the Great Lakes. There were huge oil spills off the coast of California.

All of a sudden a great many Americans had the feeling that the world was on the brink of environmental disaster. It was the perfect moment for an Establishment publisher to bring out a blockbuster environmental book. Except there was no such book in the New York publishing pipeline.

Of course my own copy center produced effort didn't have
the field completely to itself. A lot of older books about the
environment were still floating around. The difference was that
my book offered a *new* environmental vision at a time when
people were finally waking up to the need for a new vision.
More importantly, it offered a way for smart investors to profit
from the situation.

Heck, this is America. Even if the world *did* end, somebody was
going to make a packet before the final curtain descended.

I had the goods. Potential buyers were out there. I was getting
a few orders from mentions of my book in local Philadelphia
weeklies. What I really needed, though, was something with a
much stronger kick and a much wider reach to get sales into high
gear. The big break came that August when my son went off to
his freshman year at the University of Chicago.

The plan was for me to drive him to Chicago and leave the old
VW we used for the trip behind as his getting around car. Since
I was going to be there anyway, a friend who knew a talk show
host in Chicago named Pat Savage got me booked on her show.
I settled Jon in his dorm, did the TV spot, and returned to
Philadelphia with modest expectations. Modest expectations
that seemed destined not to be fulfilled. For weeks there was no
reaction whatever to my session with Pat Savage. Not a single
book order came in.

Then one morning at 6 a.m. the phone rang. Who calls at six
in the morning? A relative in the hospital? A stranger on an
all night bender dialing the wrong number? The police to say
my car was stolen and found dismembered in a public housing
project?

Annoyed, half awake, a bit nervous, I stumbled out of bed and
slouched to the phone. "I want to order your environmental
investing book," the caller exclaimed breathlessly.

Great, I thought. Just what I needed. One of my Philly pals having a little early morning fun at my expense. "Screw you," I replied, slammed down the receiver and headed back toward bed. Before I got there the phone rang again.

Pat Savage, bless her, had temporarily shelved, not trashed, my interview. Between the time it was taped and the time it actually ran, a slew of scary new environmental stories had appeared. She keyed off these stories when introducing her previously taped interview with me.

She did something else as well. Something very unusual. When she ran this interview, ordering information, including my home phone number, was put on the bottom of the screen.

Her show ran a couple of times in the morning, my interview airing each time with my telephone number listed. These airings reached an audience of several million Midwesterners, many of whom had a lively rekindled interest in all things environmental, and a fair number of whom were prepped to believe that this could be an investment opportunity as well as a global tragedy.

All that morning my phone didn't stop ringing. Since I was more awake by the time the second caller checked in, and had the good sense to ask how he got my number, I now knew the phone flood was potential book buyers and not cranks.

There was one minor problem. At noon Kay and I were leaving town for a week. Before taking off, though, we put a message on our answering machine with instructions on where to send twenty-five dollar checks to order my book.

When we returned to Philly a week later our house looked the same from the outside. There were no signs of a break-in. There was no evidence a squatter had taken possession. Nonetheless, I could not get the front door open. I pushed and I pushed. It was only after considerable effort that I got the door moved back far enough for us to squeeze inside.

Once there I came upon an awesome sight. In just a week so many envelopes had been stuffed through the mail slot that they literally kept the door from opening. I picked up one of these envelopes at random and opened it. A check fell to the floor. The note accompanying the check asked me to ship the sender a copy of my "wonderful guide" post-haste. I picked up another envelope at random and opened it. Another check and another note.

Kay and I stared at the pile of envelopes by our feet. Then we stared at each other and hugged.

The next few hours were the happiest of my gorilla publishing life. There were thousands of dollars worth of checks on the floor. I had a bank deposit stamp on my desk. Picking up and opening each envelope, removing the check inside, decorating the check's back with my bank deposit stamp, I found myself humming the Seven Dwarfs song from *Snow White*, "Hi Ho, Hi Ho, it's off to work we go."

The money was grand. Even grander was the sure and certain knowledge that I'd seen a bit further into the future than the people who were paid big bucks to do that at New York publishing houses. I had hit the seam again.

While engaged in a gorilla campaign it's usually best not to let other people know the real motivations of your actions. Explaining that you're actually engaged in a project that affirms the ability of an individual to have a say in realms that society has decreed are off-limits to anyone but certified experts gets you the fish eye at best, and in certain circumstances a forced visit to a detox center.

It's equally counter-productive to let yourself be seen as an idealist seeking to advance a noble cause without making a lot of money doing so. Such people tend to get the old head pat treatment. They are honored by power brokers in public while in private ignored or actively disdained by these same people.

In a world dominated by conventional powers, in a world where the media will only pay attention to people sporting highfalutin job titles or lengthy academic credentials, a bit of professional camouflage is often required. When pushing solar energy I pretended to head a non-existent organization called Solar Citizens of Massachusetts, and also pretended to run a faux company called Energy Marketing Associates. For credibility sake while operating as a friend of Mother Gaia, I styled myself president of another non-existent firm, this one called Environmental Economic Associates.

I never actually consulted for money or solicited consulting business. Nor, for that matter, did I ever seek or receive grants, the traditional way almost all environmental writers support themselves. The only income I ever got for my work in this field came in the form of modest sums from writing books and articles, and even lower paid adjunct teaching.

Most of the money I lived on between 1988 and 1994, in fact, had no relation to the environment. It was earned from odd jobs. I painted houses. I did telemarketing. I even delivered newspapers on weekends.

This made for some interesting juxtapositions. I was once an unpaid featured speaker, along with soon-to-be Secretary of the Interior Bruce Babbit, at a $25,000-a-head Georgetown

fundraiser, when my own annual income at the time was less
than $15,000. And I am probably the only person in American
history who was delivering The New York Times door-to-door
on weekends to make some money at the same time he was
being regularly quoted in that same newspaper and was even
writing a piece for its Sunday business section.

While this sort of thing made for a lot of laughs, it led to some
uncomfortable moments, too. I ran out of money when my son
Jon still had two years to go at the University of Chicago and it
looked for a time that he might have to drop out of school before
graduating. The little house in Center City Philadelphia where
Kay and I were living at the time with our cats, Colette and
Rambo, was also in foreclosure because my total income from
gorilla work and odd jobs didn't generate enough cash to meet
the mortgage payments.

Fortunately dumb luck, and perhaps a bit of higher power
intervention, took a hand with both these problems.

Years earlier, while still married to Suzanne and living in
Boston, I was in another one of my odd job phases. This one
involved making waterbed frames and installing assembled
versions in the homes of people who purchased them from a
shop on Charles Street.

I was not what you'd call a skilled installer. In fact, my preferred
mode of installation was to nail the liner to the inside of the
waterbed frame then anchor the liner with nails driven into the
floor—a technique that proved disastrous when water filled

mattresses subsequently sprung leaks and water seeped through the holes made by the nails.

Not surprisingly, this job didn't last very long. Before losing it, however, I made a trade that was to prove unusually propitious.

The owner of the waterbed store also sold works of art there and liked to travel to Haiti. On one of these trips he acquired a large assortment of Haitian primitives. I happened to have some extra marijuana at the time and traded it for one of these paintings.

When I brought home this acquisition it got much the same reception from Suzanne that Jack in the fairy tale got when he told his mother he had traded the family's cow for some magic beans. She pointed out, quite rightly, that this painting looked like a kindergarten production. Like many other painting by Haitian artists, it featured a little stick figure on top of a mountain with other little stick figures, and dabs of paint meant to suggest houses encircling said mountain.

Suzanne ordered it into the closet where it remained until we separated. It was one of the few things I salvaged from our separation. Thereafter, in following years, it went from closet to closet wherever I happened to be residing.

Then came the day when the bill for Jon's third year college tuition arrived. It was a killer. His previous two years at the University of Chicago had completely drained what was left of my reserves. I had no money. No steady work. Totally trashed credit. In an act of desperation I looked around the house for something, anything, of value that could be sold for cash. And there in the closet was the long forgotten Haitian primitive.

Could this closet ornament be worth something? There was nothing to lose by finding out. I took it down to a local Philadelphia auction house where an appraiser looked it over carefully, paying special attention to the artist's signature. Then

he turned the painting over and my hopes sank like a stone. I'd
forgotten that the world "Grumbacher" appeared on the rear. The
painting wasn't on canvas. It was on a slab of cheap material,
identified by the Grumbacher name, that you could buy in any
artist supply store.

"It's amazing," the appraiser said with a chuckle, "how even the
best-known Haitian primitive painters work on stuff like this."

What is he talking about, I thought? "Yes, amazing," I said
aloud.

"I could probably get you a pretty good price for this now. The
market for his work was dead for a very long time, but these
days it's coming back strong. You might want to wait, though. In
six months we'd probably get an even better price."

"My son's tuition is due," I replied honestly.

"Ah. Gotcha. We'll put her up for auction and see how she
pulls."

It turned out pulling enough to keep Jon in school for another
year.

Dumb luck certainly had a part in this incident. But so many
other pieces of 'luck' occurred about this time that I've come to
believe that Mother Gaia was looking over me in much the same
way that old Father Sol had done years earlier.

Take the case of the house in Center City Philadelphia that
Kay and I had bought after we moved from Boston. About the
same time I couldn't pay Jon's tuition bill, I couldn't cover our
housing bills. So I just stopped making mortgage payments.

My thinking here was simple. I figured three months would go
by, we'd get a letter from the bank telling us to pay up or get out,

then another three months would go by and we'd be evicted. But during these six months we'd live for free.

It wasn't an approach that filled me with joy. Then again, it didn't beat me up the way it would have done most other people.

The place was a charmer and we liked it. But hey, this wasn't the old family homestead that we had to save at all costs. It wasn't the place that grandpappy Silverstein settled in when he came from the old country, and where generations of Silversteins had lived and died since. It was just a row house whose down payment I'd made with a cash bonanza realized from the sale of another property in a different city just a few years earlier. I figured that living here free for six months was a way to recoup at least part of my down payment.

Then came the surreal dumb luck-cum-higher-power intervention. Three months after I stopped making mortgage payments we did, as anticipated, receive a notice from the bank. Rather than threatening eviction, however, it suggested we look into something called the Pennsylvania Homeowners Protection Program, and indicated that no action would be taken against us by the bank until what the notice termed a "possible solution to our problem" had been explored.

The Pennsylvania Home Owner Protection Program turned out to be the biggest government boondoggle I'd ever encountered. And I've seen plenty. It came into being as a sop to the state's coal miners. As mine after mine closed, many long-time miners and their families were left nearly destitute. Their only assets were unsalable homes on which they could no longer make mortgage payments, and a lot of clout with the Pennsylvania state legislature. These coalesced into a program found in no other state, one that paid all mortgage costs for three years, after which you were supposed to resume regular mortgage payments and repay the state for its three year subsidy.

The qualifications to take part in this program reflected its genesis. A homeowner had to have little or no regular income, few if any assets, and a poor credit rating that precluded other borrowing. All the factors, in other words, that would keep any sane lender from advancing money.

I, of course, was a perfect candidate for this program and in due course was signed up. For the next two years Kay and lived in our Center City row house without expending a dime on housing. We only moved out when the basement started to take on water during heavy rainstorms. Our free housing deal was then passed on to an artist friend of Kay who lived there free for another year.

My suspicion that a force even greater than dumb luck was at work with these housing shenanigans was reinforced by what happened after we moved from Center City. In accordance with its mandate, the program charged off the loan—in essence, excusing me from thirty-three thousand dollars of debt to the state.

But the IRS was also notified, and the $33,000 under its rules was ordinarily treated as taxable income on which federal tax was due. The one exception to this rule is that this tax obligation is excused if one happens to be legally indigent the year the debt is charged off.

Because of my work with the environment that year I was, indeed, legally indigent. The same indigence, it might be added, that along with my son's excellent academic record, helped qualify Jon for the scholarship aid he needed to finish his last year at the University of Chicago after I'd funded his third year with a dope-cum-fine-art-trade.

The final chapter of this exotic personal finance soap opera would be played out the following year when another set of highly unlikely circumstances (described in the next chapter) lifted me out of the penury bogs and into the middle class.

So here's what I've come to believe. Nobody gets really fat working for Mother Gaia. But my personal experience suggests that if you honorably serve the old girl's interests, she'll somehow get you through.

In 1992 Al Gore had a problem. He carried some awkward baggage into his run for Vice-President of the United States. Because of certain statements in his best-selling book, *Earth In The Balance*, many voters viewed him as an environmental airhead, one of those back-to-Walden-Pond granola eaters that even an increasingly pollution conscious electorate found irritating. It was this widely held perception, and the Gore campaign's efforts to change it, that for a little while in the early 1990s got me in bed again with people who for some reason the world considers wise as well as important.

It happened this way. By April 1992, scores of my articles about a new environmental economics along with my widely reviewed *The Environmental Factor* published by Longman, had appeared in print. I had become, without question, the world's most famous house painting, telemarketing, newspaper delivering environmental maven.

In terms of personal politics I have always been a left-leaning independent. Though this inclined me to dislike many of the policies of the elder George Bush who then occupied the White House, when it came to his environmental approaches I didn't find him altogether unattractive.

Bush senior wasn't a visceral screw-the-earth Reaganite. Indeed,
he seemed to possess an old money inclination to preserve
nature and keep at least some of it out of the grubby hands of
polluters. The fact that he had named William Reilly, a highly
respected environmentalist as his Secretary of the EPA, said
as much. If no one in his administration had yet twigged to the
profound implications of a new environmental economics, his
people were at least generally pragmatic and non-ideological
enough to be theoretically receptive to such thinking.

I somehow got hooked in with Bush Administration people (I
don't remember exactly how) and put forward a simple proposal.
There was to be an international environmental conference in
Rio de Janeiro early that summer. The conference would be the
largest gathering of world leaders ever, and it presented Bush
with a huge conundrum.

Suburban voters who would decide the upcoming presidential
election in this country were again clamoring for action on
the environment, which created a lot of pressure on Bush to
go to Rio. If he did go, however, he would be under enormous
pressure from other world leaders in attendance to sign on to
proposals that would alienate conservative, generally-hostile-to-
the-environment Reagan Republicans.

A large trade exhibit of environmental cleanup technologies
was scheduled for another Brazilian city, Sao Paulo, at the
same time as the Rio conference. My proposal, which I was
told was seriously considered at the highest levels of the
administration, was for Mr. Bush to attend that exhibit in Sao
Paulo, extol the virtues of the industry that was cleaning up the
world's environmental messes, and express a pro-business U.S.
determination to lead in the field, while avoiding the Rio meet
altogether, or merely dropping by for the closing ceremony.

Such a gambit would boost his standing among

environmentalists while not directly alienating the radical right since it was a business-friendly gesture. From my perspective, it would also get a sitting administration in Washington to take the first official steps toward recognizing and advancing a new environmental economics ethos.

I was told by my contact in the Bush Administration that it was a near thing. Alas, the Bushies backed away at the last minute, afraid to seem a little too soft on an issue that triggered anger on the right.

Too bad for Mr. Bush. This simple gesture might actually have been enough to win him the election that November. Too bad for the rest of us, too. It would have saved us from a Bill Clinton presidency.

But I'm getting a little bit ahead of myself here.

After this brief flirtation with Bush the Elder, how did I get mixed up with Al Gore and the same type of bubbleheads who had undermined my solar energy efforts fifteen years earlier?

In April 1992 the Wall Street Journal ran an article of mine on its Op Ed page. I wasn't exactly a stranger to the Journal by then. In the 1970s, while purporting to be an expert on tax shelters (believe me, you don't want to know how that came about), I was quoted on its front page about investment prospects for oil drillers. Later in that decade, while carving out a brief and unsuccessful career as a prose financial humorist, a couple of my spoofs turned up on the Journal's editorial page. My self-created credentials as an environmental economist also earned mentions for my environmental investing guide in other sections of the Journal during 1990 and 1991.

My appearance on the paper's Op Ed page in April 1992 nonetheless contained ideas that were generally new to the Journal and its readers. Pollution, I wrote, was just another name for waste, so the more efficient a business became, the less wasteful, the less it polluted. New technologies almost always were less polluting than the technologies they replaced, so greening was a mark of economic evolution. There was a competitive advantage for companies that sold greener products, especially in richer countries. Today's pollution was tomorrow's profit deadening bottom line liability. By 1992 I could write stuff like this in my sleep.

It was the closer of this piece, however, that really attracted attention. With half-an-eye still on the Bush camp, I asked rhetorically why 'the environment' was still considered an anti-business issue, when new environmental economic realities so obviously made it a business-friendly issue.

The Bush people didn't bite. But a nervous Gore campaign jumped on the idea like a hungry carp. To them I appeared a business-savvy environmentalist that even the Wall Street Journal took seriously, exactly what the electoral politics of the time demanded that Al Gore pretend to be. I was contacted the same day the piece appeared in the Journal and proceeded to become an unpaid environmental media beard for Al Gore during the 1992 presidential election campaign.

Alright. I'll admit it. At first I was flattered by the attention. For months it seemed that every time the Gore campaign got a query about how environment-related factors affected the economy, the caller was referred to me. Articles of mine on a new environmental economics were being published every week. I was quoted in magazines and newspapers almost on a daily basis. I was getting booked for a slew of radio interviews.

It was fun. Occasionally it was even funny.

Like the time I was being followed around for awhile by a New York Times reporter named Keith Schneider. I used the time to throw out some of my favorite catch phrases, including one that went: "If pollution really created wealth, Poland would be the richest country in Europe." The following Sunday, in the paper's News Of The Week section, Keith wrote an article in which that phrase was attributed to Al Gore.

Gore in print was channeling my thinking. The New York Times had become my medium. I delivered that edition of The Times on my regular weekend newspaper route. A real hoot.

Though flattered by this short-lived bout of fame, I was also astonished at the success of this gorilla action. I was, after all, an indigent odd jobber, unaffiliated with any organization, completely lacking professional qualifications about a subject with enormous intrinsic complexity. Beyond that, I had never done any research in the field beyond reading newspapers and quoting people who agreed with me while attacking those who didn't.

I wasn't a hypocrite. I truly believed in what I was writing. But it was all based on common sense.

The important thing at this juncture, as I saw it, was to get the priorities right. Environmental considerations should not be a part of economic thinking. Economic thinking should be built around preserving and protecting the natural environment. The environment isn't a part of us. We're a part of it.

Until that basic, obvious, transcendentally important ordering of things was worked into economic thinking and behavior, things had to be diddled a bit. In the past countless people had ignored or actively disdained good environmental behavior because they believed polluting created wealth. If countless people could be made to believe that good environmental behavior created wealth, appropriate decisions would follow naturally.

Once I got this ball rolling the right way, I felt certain that others with far more resources, credentials, and positions of power than what I had at my disposal would fill out the canvas and I could move on to other things. I was pretty tired of delivering newspapers on the weekends to make ends meet.

My work with the Gore campaign lasted only a few months. That was more than enough for me. When it over I felt like taking a hundred year shower.

At first it was the little things. Peripheral characters associated with the campaign in mysterious ways started being overly nice to me. I would say things that were egregiously stupid and they would agree. I would tell awful jokes and they would fall over themselves laughing. They hinted that they had read all my past environmental writing and let me know they thought my style ranked with Melville.

And then there were those suggestive questions. Did I need this or that to help with my work? What sort of position did I envision for myself after the election?

There were gifts, or offers of gifts, as well. One day an expensive new fax machine was delivered to my home by FedEx, along with a note from a Washington-based public relations firm thanking me for the good work I was doing "for the cause." No cause was specified, but the sender's business card was attached to the machine so I would know who was on my side during the great coming struggle.

I was inclined to throw the fax into a closet and keep it as memento, in the space recently occupied by a Haitian primitive. But Kay was adamant about the need to return it along with a note saying I don't accept gifts for my work with the campaign.

Kay is a woman who expects a guy to live up to the ideals he espouses. No wonder we're always broke.

The sucking up, the little gifts, the endless blatant attempts to get closer to someone like me who appeared to be moving up in the pecking order, made me very uncomfortable. It put me in mind of those lines in Shakespeare's *Julius Caesar*, lines describing people who fawn on you and hug you hard and after scandal you. Which, as it happened, was exactly how these people behaved toward me a few months later, after the Clinton-Gore team had oozed its way into power with help from a media savvy, big-eared, deep-pocket Texas blowhard named Ross Perot.

My own severance from a newly elected Clinton-Gore Administration and the folks it would come to flagrantly front

came about this way. I was invited to speak at a $25,000-a-head
fundraiser hosted by Gore's campaign chairman, Colorado
Senator Tim Wirth. The two other speakers on the program were
a Princeton professor hyping some kind of safer nuclear power
technology, and Bruce Babbit, who would go on to become
Secretary of the Interior.

The Princeton guy bombed. Very few people in this audience
of well-heeled old-line environmentalists had any sympathy
for nuclear. As for Babbit, he made the mistake of ending a
pretty good talk about the defects of the elder George Bush's
environmental policies by offering a few examples of companies
he said were actually making money doing the right thing by
Mother Gaia—as if doing the right thing by the old girl and
making money in the process were an unusual combination. It
was precisely the wrong line to take just before one of my own
talks about a new environmental economics.

Not deliberately, but unmistakably, I proceeded to make Babbit
look foolish. After an historical overview and a brief outline
of new environmental economics basics, I jumped from major
industry to major industry showing how each was already being
restructured into greener configurations by new market-based
imperatives.

Babbit stood in the back of the room glowering like a man ticked
off because he hadn't brought along his .30-06. I have that effect
on some people.

The audience loved my rap, however—though most probably
saw it more as a clever ruse to con voters long enough to get
their men into power than as a genuine new way to view the
business-environmental nexus. I was, in any case, lionized after
the talk and later at a Georgetown reception and dinner.

It was at this reception that a small, wiry, expensively dressed
woman introduced herself. She said her name was Rhona. As we

spoke I noticed that several people near us leaned closer to catch a word or two.

Later that evening one of the campaign people took me aside and asked if I knew the woman I had been speaking with.

"She said her name was Rhona," I replied.

He laughed. "Rhona is a *very* big contributor. A *very* heavy hitter. Congratulations. You're in." And he gave me a playful pat on the shoulder.

It seemed I had just scored in a game whose rules I didn't understand and whose other players I didn't know or have a wish to know. Lucky me.

Shortly after the election I received an invitation to a meeting in a Manhattan lawyer's office. Rhona's lawyer. I assumed this meet would have something to do with the new administration's environmental policies and priorities. Not exactly, it turned out.

The address and the layout let you know right off that the lawyer who presided here was big-time and well-connected. If that didn't impress, one of the people at the conference room table where we got seated whispered the names of some of his other clients, a list that included several deposed foreign presidents and prime ministers. It seems such representation is now a legal specialty. Like asbestos litigation.

The pleader himself made a brief cameo appearance, perhaps as a special sign of favor to Rhona. He was a graying man of middle years, a tad overweight, wearing thick-lensed glasses and sporting that year's symbol of I-don't-give-a-shit-what-you-think wearing apparel, yellow suspenders. He slowly and obviously scrutinized each of us at the table with that piercing gaze lawyers and police detectives practice in front of a mirror every morning—the one designed to let you know that all your dirty little secrets are known to the gazer. This done, he turned the floor over to Rhona and left the room, leaving behind a junior lawyer person who would take notes like a stenographer and likely bill at rates ten times as large.

Rhona, it seemed, had a Great Idea, and those of us around the table—a couple of representatives from environmental organizations, a few flinty eyed Washington bureaucratic types, our lady lawyer stenographer and me — were there to tell her how great it was. The idea was for something called 'Peace Bonds.'

When Rhona first emoted the words "peace bonds" I was confused. We were in an American lawyer's office and peace bonds are the term used for restraining orders in Canadian courts. Her peace bonds notion was something very different, though. Peace bonds, as she explained, were supposed to be like war bonds, but instead of raising money by the government to fight a war, these government bonds would be used to invest in environmental technologies.

I never did understand all the fine points here because they were not spelled out at the meeting. Which wasn't very surprising because the idea was silly. You want to establish a sector fund to invest in these technologies, sure, why not. There were already some in existence, another one wouldn't hurt. But one run by the government, with public-backed funding, which appeared to be Rhona's idea? This was so, so, decades-out-of-date.

Japan's targeting of certain industries this way had worked well for a time, but was clearly unraveling by the early 1990s. Indeed,

Japan had fallen into recession in 1989, a recession from which it would not exit for many long and difficult years.

Why emulate that country's outdated growth model? Why get into government-supported targeting at all when a free market would easily provide all the capital needed for environmental technologies if the market were appropriately goosed by a heavy dose of new environmental economics jawboning, a modest tightening of the regulatory screws, and most helpful, large government purchases of environmentally appropriate products and systems?

It was Rhona's show day, however, and I didn't want to ruin it for her. Though goodness knows I had a very good reason to do so.

Here we were in New York City, the world capital of good kosher deli, and for lunch instead of ordering in corned beef, pastrami, and half sour pickles for guests who had traveled from half-a-dozen other cities to hear her ridiculous peace bond twaddle, we got this nouveau veggie stuff on pita bread with granola dressing. Clearly, Rhona was a woman who had lost her way on several fronts.

A few days later, after I'd shared a good laugh about peace bonds with some campaign acquaintances, one of whom apparently felt obliged to pass along my views, I got the inevitable call from Rhona.

"I hear you don't think much of my concept."

It was a critical moment. A moment when aside from environmental considerations a more politic person would have hummed, hawed and hedged, because that peace bond meeting was obviously just a prelude to divvying up some successful campaign's spoils. Except that gorillas aren't very good at hedging and hawing, and this gorilla wasn't in it for the spoils.

Besides, there were those sandwiches foisted on us at the lunch
in the lawyer's lair. Those arugula, organic tomato, sprouts and
cucumber creations awash in ultra virgin oil on whole wheat
pitas served with iced tea (iced tea!), in lieu of honest humped-
back corned beef specials with Russian dressing flanked by over-
salted chips made moist and succulent with the juicy runoff of
half sour pickles and washed down with a Dr. Brown's Celeray.

Yes, I'm a gorilla. But when it comes to eating I'm not a beast
of the forest. I have needs, too, This sort of mistreatment isn't
easily overlooked.

More than anything else, though, what determined my response
to Rhona was my personal feelings toward the woman. I kind
of liked her. She reminded me of times long past, of early
adolescent evenings under the boardwalk in Rockaway Beach,
on a blanket resting on mounds of cool sand, listening to the
first cum cries of a rabbi's daughter as I labored vigorously but
ineptly to decipher an unfamiliar anatomy. For triggering that
memory, I owed this woman the truth.

"Peace bonds are a stupid idea," I said. "And you should have
ordered corned beef for our lunch."

No, I didn't expect to be thanked for my honesty. An
experienced gorilla knows the likely reaction when he shits in
someone else's nest.

Rhona slammed down the phone and I never heard from
her again. Nor did I ever hear again from anyone in the new
administration in Washington. Nor from environmental
organization types with whom I'd worked so long and hard
during the 1992 food fight without any sort of compensation.
The latter, who having hugged me hard so recently, upon
learning that I had dissed a big campaign contributor on whom

they wished to feed, now saw the wisdom of scandalizing me.

It was like a dream. It seemed a perfect gorilla project. I had appeared on the environmental scene from nowhere, hit the seam, made a splash in a realm where I had no business being except that the people already there were missing something both important and obvious. Now I could move on.

There didn't seem to be any reason not to move on. I felt certain that some version of my own new environmental economics would become the official, high profile policy of the new Clinton-Gore Administration, promoted by people who were convinced they had invented it. Like the old soldier described (if not exactly emulated) by General Douglas MacArthur, I could now just fade away.

I could maybe start making a few extra bucks again working more hours with Joe and his Group W Bench house painters. A revolving Felliniesque collection of interesting and entertaining characters that at various times included a sculptor waiting for his next grant from the Pew Foundation, a former special forces trooper, a couple of longshorewomen, some motorcycle bikers, and the occasional skilled craftsman like Joe himself.

These were great people to work with. People with valuable knowledge for any indigent urban dweller. They knew, for example, where the local chop shops were located, how to get there before your stolen car was dismembered and on its way to a port in the South China Sea, who to mention to the chop shop operator to ensure a reasonable transaction could be consummated. Valuable information like that.

I was the oldest person in the crew and by far the least skilled,
the coffee gofer, the dropped paint scrapper upper. Joe claimed
I was one of his two personal charities. The other one was
a Vietnam burnout, a guy you gave two beers and sent up a
shaky thirty-foot ladder on a windy day to paint an otherwise
unreachable area near the roof because he no longer understood
the meaning of fear or pretty much anything else.

House painting with Joe was hard work but the time passed
quickly because the company was so good. My fellow workers
were nothing like the stereotypes my recent Beltway associates
invariably referred to as "Joe Sixpacks." Most of Joe's crew
might be making art one day and house painting another,
entering graduate school one year and pumping gas or bumming
rides cross-country a year later. Their conversation was not only
more interesting than the gossipy back-biting and suck-up of
the Beltway hacks I'd met in Clinton-Gore land, it was more
politically sophisticated, more focused on real world issues,
more filled with intellectual content.

We listened to both righty Rush Lambaugh and lefty Irv Homer
on the radio, traded tips on how to get new Social Security
numbers and credit cards for a pet, argued philosophy, discussed
books, drank Sam Adams beer in Friday afternoons, Joe's treat.
When we did jobs in churches, someone diligently painted 666
in out-of-the-way corners where the light was bad.

These were people who made you proud to live in Philly—
or anywhere else for that matter, places where folks had an
appropriate disrespect for the established order.

Alas, my pleasantly disrespectful and solvency-solving sojourn
with the Group W Bench house painting gang didn't last long.
Instead of my new environmental economics becoming a
showpiece of a freshly minted Clinton-Gore Administration, this
administration immediately started flying off in wrong directions

when it came to Mother Gaia. I was obliged as a matter of honor to lay down the brush again and reach for the gorilla gear.

How did the Clinton-Gore Administration fail when it came to the environment? Let me count the ways.

It failed in its first two years in office, while it still had an environment-friendly Democratic Congress, to push for meaningful legislation in this field. Thereafter, because this administration's own bungling had brought a yahoo, anti-environment Republican Congress to power, no meaningful legislation was possible.

It completely de-balled the environmental movement. During the presidential campaign of 1992 every poll showed the environment was second only to the economy as the political issue voters most cared about. By the election of 1996 it wasn't even on the political radar. Bill Clinton oozed sympathy for the movement, felt its pain, sported a flannel shirt on Earth Day, while Al Gore fed movement leaders heavy thoughts, fancy meals, and little else in Blair House, his official vice presidential residence.

Such cheap tricks kept environmental groups from criticizing the administration. Which in turn convinced the public that the environment was at last in good hands. Which in turn led to a lack of the popular outrage of the kind that in past years generated real progress. Which translated into loss of financial support for environment groups. Which made these groups increasingly dependent on deep pocket types whose own primary concerns were stock and bond manipulation packaged as "globalization," wrangling sleepovers in the Lincoln bedroom, and keeping people who fronted for their real interests in power.

Politically speaking, by Clinton-Gore's second term, the environmental movement had become just another sucked dry support prop for a toothless, scandal-ridden, Wall Street-enabling administration.

What should have been the primary environmental aim of Clinton-Gore? A much expanded, well articulated version of my new environmental economics. A version that fully and finally fused in the popular consciousness environmental well-being and economic well-being. A version that would thereafter make it terribly difficult to 'make the hard choices' between the economy and the environment because such choices in the real world were no longer really necessary.

That's what should have been done but wasn't done. Once I was axed from the scene, Clinton-Gore had no clear, coherent, well articulated new environmental vision, just a mishmash of programs and initiatives with no central focus or discernible, clearly defined purpose.

Ultimately, from out of this chaos, would arise the two main approaches that were to define Clinton-Gore's own defective environmental thinking—emissions credit trading and sustainable development theorizing—a dreadful duo that together for long years largely ended the role of the U.S. government as a positive force for environmental improvement.

Emissions credit trading is one of those ideas everyone instinctively knows is stupid but which are kept alive by special interests until the time when in spite of the idea's foolishness it dovetails with the proclivities of those in power. The 1990s were a decade when anything that could be packaged as a 'free market solution' could turn Beltway types loose-lipped and pliable. It was thus a snap for promoters of emission credit trading—a mix of Wall Streeters wanting new products to peddle, and old-line polluters anxious to put off their own environmental reckonings a few more years—to bill this turkey as a "free market solution to pollution."

Emissions trading allows polluters to buy out of cleaning up their own messes by paying others to mess less. Or to put this another way, it lets polluters pay others for the right to continue legally polluting themselves. The free market mechanism supposedly at work here is that companies able to reduce pollution most efficiently and at the lowest cost will be rewarded to doing so, and the end result will be the largest possible pollution reduction at the lowest possible overall cost.

To get a feel for how intrinsically preposterous this approach actually is, imagine if it were applied in a program to reduce serious crime. Here, people who haven't committed any Class A felonies in the last two years would be given 'crime credits' they could sell to people who find it temporarily inconvenient to stop stealing, raping, and killing. If this strikes you as a great way to reduce serious crime, you probably think emission credit trading is a great way to reduce pollution.

In the real world, companies rarely if ever reduce their pollution output in order to create saleable emission credits. It's not a money-making proposition. What happens instead is that to stay competitive they upgrade their operations by buying and using new equipment. This new equipment generally pollutes less then the equipment it replaces. An unintended byproduct of this upgrading is the creation of a faux-asset—an emissions credit—

which can then be sold to a member of the let-me-keep-polluting league. In other situations, a big polluter might buy already existing forest tracts whose trees absorb pollutants, and claim such ownership excuses it from cutting its own emissions.

And then there was that other Clinton-Gore chimera— sustainable development theory—an approach that stands in relation to my new environmental economics as the proverbial committee designed camel stands in relation to a horse.

My own writing in this field describes a natural, inevitable synthesis of environmental and economic well-being brought about by technology and market forces as economies evolve further and further from their high-polluting Industrial Revolution roots. This approach is an easy to understand mix of industrial ecology and common sense. It presents good environmental behavior as a tool of individual managers seeking more profit and a competitive edge; a spur to creativity and efficiency; a pragmatic and immediate way to improve company bottom lines and animate national economies.

Sustainable development theory is about the future not the present. It's a son-of-Marx approach to environmental improvement involving central planning by governments. It's a head game and time waster for international agency bureaucrats, academics, and smarmy representatives of the world's biggest polluters, the latter rapping the rap and picking up the tab.

My new environmental economics aimed to bring environmentalism into real world thinking. Sustainable development theory took it back to the campus.

What made this distinction so personally painful was that it was so familiar to me. In the 1970s a Democratic administration was chained to an approach that sought to promote solar energy in the mid-term and long-term, even though some very long proven solar technologies could have been intelligently promoted immediately with wonderful consequences for both the economy and the natural environment. Twenty years later another Democratic administration was promoting a long-term view of why good environmental behavior was a good economic idea instead of recognizing and promoting the fact that such behavior already was.

Were these people so smart that they were incapable of learning the obvious? Would they never stop visualizing the future and just open their eyes to the present?

Apparently not

Even before emissions credit trading and sustainable development theory, the Gog and Magog of Clinton-Gore environmental policy, had fully risen from the pit, I knew where this administration was headed when it came to the environment. It was déjà vu all over again. The same kind of people—maybe even the same people—who had done so much to harm Father Sol in the 1970s were cranking up to do it again to Mother Gaia in the1990s.

Their basic flaws as policy-makers were so, so obvious: Confusing intelligence with imagination; wealth with ability; pronouncements with progress; complexity with comprehensiveness; personal interests with public interests; academic schemes with visions.

Very soon after the 1992 election I knew who they were and why they acted the way they did. I also knew this battle was destined to be much less successful than my earlier gorilla raid on the

Northeast Solar Energy Center. There I had a single, easily
recognizable target and was only outnumbered a hundred to one
in terms of personnel and a few thousand to one when to came to
financial resources. Here, the target was an entire administration
in Washington and its prime supporters. With luck I might land a
few shots, but there wasn't the slightest chance I'd even stagger
the beast.

There were a number of personal factors working against me
now as well. I was older. I was even poorer. I had a home in
foreclosure and problems paying my son's tuition.

I nonetheless slouched forth to do what I could for Gaia
in a futile attempt to save the old girl from the corrosive
ministrations of Clinton-Gore. My first blow landed in the form
of an opinion piece in the Sunday Business Section of the New
York Times.

It was a modest and retrained bit of criticism that seemed
appropriate inasmuch as the administration was still only a few
months old. Its main thrust, in fact, was simply to note that
while the ascension to power of a strongly pro-military Reagan
a dozen years earlier led to huge military appropriation increases
in the federal budget and was a boom for defense contractors,
the ascension of a supposedly pro-environment Clinton-
Gore seemed not to be leading to a comparable growth in
environmental spending and a boom for pollution cleanup firms.

Did I get a slew of calls from environmental groups thanking
me for this well meant goosing? Heck, no. Instead what I
got were nasty letters published in subsequent issues of The
Times from consultant types doing a suck up defense of the
new Administration in hopes of landing contracts. From
environmental groups you might think had a duty to hold
Clinton-Gore's feet to the fire on green issues in payment for
the electoral support they had provided, I got no response at all.
They remained loyal and silent during the following eight years

as their supposed champions nickeled and dimed their interests when bothering to pay attention to them at all.

With friends like these, enemies of the environment were just add-ons.

So it went. In the following years I had dozens of articles published in high profile media challenging Clinton-Gore to do something serious and useful in this field, or criticizing the worse-than-useless things this administration was actually doing. By the time the 1996 presidential election rolled around I was hyping the candidacy of Bob Dole on National Public Radio and elsewhere.

I thought Dole might actually do a better job on the environment. Some of the biggest advances made on environmental issues had been made under Republican presidents, from Theodore Roosevelt to Richard Nixon to George Bush the Elder. I also believed an environmental movement freed of links to Clinton-Gore might regain some of its fighting spirit.

"Dole and a Democratic congress," was my personal election pitch that year. "Throw all the bums out, in both congress and the administration."

Nothing I did or tried to do had any effect whatever. Bill and Al were reelected with the help of a now pathetic, spineless environmental movement that asked nothing for its wholehearted support other than a few tickets to the second inaugural ball.

I finally threw in the towel.

Now I was truly free again. Alas, I was also broke, sick, and apparently headed for a profoundly uncomfortable dotage in a third tier trailer park outside Biloxi.

Then things in my personal life took a sharp turn for the better.

VI.
Final Pre-G Training:
A Clint Eastwood Gorilla In St. James Palace

I'm looking back again at some personal experiences that helped shape my gorilla view of life.

After I left Munich and Betsy, I traveled with Suzanne for awhile in a used VW bus furnished with a mattress, a spare tire, and little else. In Barcelona we traded down to a small motorbike and hopped a ferry to Ibiza, the largest island in the Balearic group located between Spain and Africa. From there we got on another boat and traveled to the smallest island in the group, Formentera.

Like almost every other place in Europe with a beach in the mid-1960s this little isle was experiencing an influx of newly rich German tourists. Though happily, it was still not yet inundated, and not yet transformed into a typical tourist paradise. In fact, it retained a fair number of surreal elements, some charming, some scary, some peculiarly Spanish in a Cervantes kind of way.

Spain was then still a dictatorship under the awful tutorship of Francisco Franco. But it was also in desperate need of tourists to prop up a very weak economy. Formentera's official law enforcers, the Civil Guardia, nasty young guys in terribly uncomfortable wool uniforms, with black plastic triangular hats, carrying 1930s-vintage rifles, were therefore ordered not to interfere with naughty tourist goings on. They spent their time instead looking at bikini-clad foreign women through binoculars, drooling but not daring to touch.

Suzanne and I took up residence in Formentara's only windmill. Most of the island was long, narrow and flat. But on one end rose a plateau. The windmill was at the very end of this plateau, overlooking the sea.

It had an artesian well that we couldn't use because the last resident of the mill, an American girl, decided to bath in it. The farmer who owned the mill lived nearby let us use his for drinking water. He also gave us free tomatoes and other fruits he raised. Nice man.

Our outhouse was a little stone affair next to the mill. You could watch little green salamanders climbing its walls while you did your business. Ropes running from the mill's blades to the ground kept the blades from turning. Mice ran up and down the ropes after dark. At least I think they were mice.

A circular staircase running along the inside walls of the mill led from the ground level where we ate, to the second level where we slept, to a small third level with a tiny window that let you look out at a perfectly blue-green sea in the daytime and a perfectly black sky with a trillion stars at night.

By a stroke of luck— I'm not sure whether good or bad — while we lived there a floating gaggle of international hippies-cum-lost souls that gathered in out of the way places like Portuguese Goa and Machu Picchu in the Andes this season descended on Formentera. In the evenings we joined them, sitting around huge fires, passing around pipes with various contents and pills of different colors, happily partaking of the mindlessness that resulted.

Then things changed quickly. An American ex-pat who had lived on the island for years did something incredibly stupid. His drug-fueled cavorting with two much younger American women didn't end before dawn. Children passing close to his house on their way to school heard and perhaps saw naughty things going on inside.

In a Spain, where a surprising amount of any kind of personal behavior was permitted in private, this was an unforgivable no-no. A red line that should never have been crossed. The ex-pat was hauled away later that same day to a place you didn't want to know about in Franco-era Spain.

The island's Civil Guardia nasties were about to be unchained. We were off to Ibiza a few days later, and on to England thereafter.

England in the late 1960s was a curious mix. It still hadn't fully recovered economically from WW II. Its people stayed warm by slipping shillings into pay radiators, and were perpetually grumpy by virtue of being forced to use waxy toilet tissue embossed with the London Transport logo. Drinking cheap, warm beer to excess in pubs was the chief national pastime.

Culturally, though, London when we arrived was beginning to percolate. The music scene, greatly animated by American black artists on tour, was churning out groups like the Beatles and Rolling Stones. The Lady Jane boutique had just opened on Carnaby Street. The cinema had turned angry and poignant, or in the case of the Beatles *Yellow Submarine* released in 1968, innovative and great fun. Monte Python would start appearing on BBC in 1969.

Through a friend we knew in Munich, Suzanne and I landed an apartment in Bloomsbury that we shared with a BBC music producer. He always seemed to have friends dropping by who had 'come down' from Oxford or Cambridge. It was my introduction to the English class scene, whose very top and bottom I would soon explore more fully when I got a job cleaning St. James Palace.

My first real work gig in London, however, was as a model. Someone introduced me to a photographer who did paperback book covers. He offered me a job posing for his latest project, portraying the Man With No Name, the bounty hunter character in Clint Eastwood's spaghetti westerns.

On my favorite one of these book covers, *A Dollar To Die For*, now proudly hanging on my bedroom wall, I'm ill-shaven, puffing on a short cheroot, holding an old-style six-shooter, the photo's lighting accentuating my overall dangerous look. A look easy to understand once you read the book's plot on the back cover.

Here was described The Man With No Name's quest for lost gold once owned by Maximilian, former emperor of Mexico. A quest that pits him against a deadly trio — the courtly but duplicitous Count de Cabronet, the rapacious Tuco the Terrible, and Pinky Roebuck, a very badly mannered albino Apache.

After the modeling work petered out, lacking working papers needed by foreigners to get any decent work, I took whatever I could get. I soon became a char, a housecleaner, the English class system's equivalent of India's untouchables.

The charring agency that employed me had no discernible standards. Heroin was legal in England in these years if you a prescription, and all my fellow employees were users. All except for me and a young guy named Pat who preferred LSD, and had his own druggie's view of reality.

I remember one time we were working together, cleaning a house, and I asked Pat what other jobs he'd done.

"I was an usher in a movie house for awhile," he said. "I saw the Beatles' *Yellow Submarine* 235 times."

I thought it was a sad recollection and was about to sympathize when he added with a faraway look of pleasure: "It was that good."

One day the charring agency got a call from the housekeeper of the Queen's Secretary, Lord Charteris. The poor woman had broken her arm. Help was needed in St. James palace with cleaning chores.

Sending someone to meet this need the agency owner could choose among heroin addicts, Pat, or me. I was his default.

Which is how I came to clean the apartment of the Queen's Secretary in St. James Palace. And how I got an up-close peek at the very acme of this class-ridden society from my own place at the very bottom of the upstairs-downstairs ladder.

It was to my mind a curious experience, filled with little incidents that struck me as not just outdated but very un-American. The ambience here oozed social ossification, everything and everyone fixed in settled and accepted roles.

In retrospect it was a personal foretaste of where we appear headed today in this country. Back then it was something an American like myself could happily fancy we had managed to transcend.

I left England on Guy Fawkes Day 1968 on an Icelandic Airline flight that did a stopover in Reykjavik, Iceland's capital, where I watched the final returns of the 1968 election in a bar at the airport in company with two green berets. Richard Nixon was to be President. America was about the change in big ways.

As was I.

Back in New York I got work writing for underground pubs like Screw and business pubs like Ralph Ginzburg's Moneysworth newsletter. I was the first editor of the latter, and the first to be fired from that position. Ginzburg fired a lot.

Rather than look for other work immediately, my little family opted to collect my unemployment insurance on another island. Nantucket. Our timing was perfect. We arrived there at the very end of the island's summer tourist season.

We were thus able to rent a lovely house for deeply discounted off-season peanuts. I was soon collecting my unemployment checks at the American Legion Hall because there were no state offices on the island.

To pick up extra cash I did off-the-books construction work. I also supplemented the family diet by writing angry letters to food packagers complaining about bugs in their cereals and soups. A case of the falsely disparaged product usually came back a short time later.

If complaining could generate such a response, I reasoned, compliments would get even better returns. So I wrote the president of Pepperidge Farms saying I saw God while eating one of his Milano cookies.

He sent back a personal thank you note but no cookies. Live and learn.

It was prudent for people like myself, even with a family in tow, to leave Nantucket by Memorial Day, the start of the tourist season. Our off-season construction labor was no longer needed, and our presence might offend the better sort of visitors about to arrive.

I'd been alerted to the exact time to start packing. It was when a new young guy would suddenly appear on the island, hot to buy some smoke, and especially anxious to do business with 'Mr. Big.' The island's Mr. Big the season I was there, the major marijuana supplier, was a kid who drove down to Kentucky in an old pick up truck, sneaked into a farmer's field after dark where he'd planted his own crop of Kentucky Blue, harvested the weed, dried it in a Lexington laundromat, drove it back to Nantucket in a plastic garbage bag, and smoked half his stash himself to calm the jitters the adventure generated.

The DEA guy hot to meet Mr. Big arrived on schedule. We left before he made (or didn't make) his big drug bust. From Nantucket Suzanne, Jon, and myself were off to Boston.

Where my gorilla days would soon begin.

VII.
Putting Poems Where They Belong
(The Gorilla Turns To Rhyme)

I'd never especially liked poetry. Except for brief and forced encounters in high school and college, I'd rarely read it and never went out of my way to hear someone recite it. It was thus passing strange that I was to emerge as a fairly famous purveyor of light verse, and then go on to spend considerable time in a food fight involving poetry with the people who control both this country's poetry media and its opinion pages.

As is usually the case, these gorilla actions had an odd genesis. After those serious health problems touched on in the last chapter (alright, if you must know, by this time I'd had two bouts of cancer along with open heart surgery, a couple of bypasses and a mini-stroke) I figured I was going to croak in the near future.

My son was by now married and doing his own career number in Chicago, and my life associate Kay Wood was a highly regarded fine artist moving into graphic novels. Neither was rich, however, and both in my reckoning deserved some monetary recompense for the shit I'd put them through over the years. Since the path of the gorilla had given me an estate that largely consisted of soiled linen and overdue Visa bills, I figured it was finally time to make a few bucks to help secure their post-me futures.

So I did something I hadn't done in decades. I sent out resumes in response to employment ads I saw one Sunday in the classified section of the New York Times. Two resumes, to be exact, and one of these landed me a job with Bloomberg Financial News in Princeton, New Jersey.

Why I was hired was something of a mystery, not only to me but to anyone else who knew me at the time. I was 55. I had no history of working for a similar firm or any large firm. I also didn't bother disguising my general antipathy to corporate culture.

On the other hand I did have a lot of business and financial writing experience and a national reputation in a few specialties. Financial media of all kinds was also expanding rapidly in 1990s while the supply of media talent with appropriate backgrounds lagged demand. And there were, of course, those other qualifications I brought to the job.

The man who introduced me to the Bloomberg staff after I'd been hired made a point of noting I was a former military policeman and the author of *Planet of Financial Planners*. Few of his younger staffers had done any soldiering, which somehow made this first credential seem oddly appealing. As for the latter credential—he must have been one of the six people who actually read this massively ignored work of satire.

But there was a problem. Just prior to getting this job I had written a very different book, *The Controller's Environmental Compliance Manual,* for another financial services publisher. The person I worked for on this project liked my work, and said he planned to hire me to write and edit a newsletter for controllers that his company would soon launch. It was when this newsletter gig didn't come through for several months that I took the Bloomberg job. Then the newsletter opportunity finally was offered and I was in a quandary.

Here I'd been a freelance indigent who suddenly had two high-paying offers on the table from companies that were competitors. Obviously I couldn't do both. On the other hand...

The solution was to have Kay, my fine arts life companion, whose knowledge of controllership roughly equaled her knowledge of Sanskrit, do the call around work for the newsletter with me doing most of the writing and editing in the evenings after a day's work at Bloomberg. This solution had the effect of converting our prior combined four-figure annual income into a six-figure income. Since our spending habits barely changed during the years we practiced this dual legerdemain, it allowed me to retire from the Bloomberg fold in less than five years.

During these years at Bloomberg I still managed a few gorilla raids. I also began producing work that would one day make me America's foremost financial poet.

A digression here with gorilla overtones. Before my financial poetry writing at Bloomberg began there was the financial music — if music it was. More specifically, there was a company of sorts called Financial Harmonics that I created as a sideline with the help of a few young geniuses.

Bloomberg had a bunch of these brilliant young people in-house. The company was highly regarded in its field, making it a wonderful resume addition, and its benefits (at least while I worked there) were great. Just the sort of things that attracted the 1990s best and brightest twenty-somethings, though truth be told, they didn't mean squat to me when I was in my twenties and out to piss on the Establishment, not feed off it.

Along with writing financial news stories, some of these twenty-somethings worked with the company's patented analytic programs. These programs allowed users to perform high colonic analysis on all manner of financial instruments using exotic mathematical modeling techniques.

At least I think that's what they did. Heck, I could barely turn on the fancy computer they gave me. I even had trouble adjusting the eight hundred dollar ergonomically engineered chair they gave us to sit in.

Fortunately, as the oldest person on the staff, there was always a sympathetic young person there to get me going. And once I was underway I performed editing marvels inasmuch as I had, for some reason, a strange ability to turn the largely incomprehensible gibberish sent my way into some variant of understandable English.

It also didn't take me long to realize that almost no one in this corporation (and I suspect large corporations generally) did a lot of what I thought of as real work. They might come in early and stay late, they might stare at the machines on their desks with the focused concentration of sub commanders on a torpedo run, but their actual output of finished product was piddling.

When you're self-employed as I had been for so many years there's no one to screw with low production other than yourself. But when you're working on a corporate farm the usual reward for completing old projects too quickly is getting a flood of new ones to do. Thus it was that I was soon recognized by management as a surprisingly good hire—while being asked by my workmates to ease up a bit and not rock the boat.

One day, on a break, I happened to be talking to a bright young guy named Rameen who was studying Persian poetry at nearby Princeton University when not doing analytics for Bloomberg. There's a pathological romanticism to such poetry I found kind of interesting. Sentiments like: I'd happily drive a serrated kitchen knife deep into my thorax if you'd but deign to look my way. Coming across such thinking gives one important insights into contemporary Middle Eastern politics.

Anyway, for no particular reason, I happened to mention a short story I'd written a decade or two earlier titled "Composer's Market." The story's basic premise was that if you changed the charted movements of stocks into musical notation, and a person was somehow attuned to this notational mode, then upon 'hearing' these past movements this person could compose a few bars ahead. These composed-ahead bars could then be turned back into movements on a stock chart, and you would know where the stock's price was headed.

"I think I know people who could do that," said Rameen. And Financial Harmonics was born.

Rameen was easily able to change past movements of stocks as recorded on the Bloomberg system into a form he thought could be turned into musical notation. He made these movements more sophisticated by adding a stock's trading volumes and a few other bells and whistles.

Rameen had a lot of time to do this kind of thing after working hours because in spite of having a wonderfully sensitive face, coming from a rich and prominent Iranian family, being a superb tennis player, and being able to recite Persian love poetry so drenched in romantic excess it could bring a jar of pickles to orgasm, he couldn't get a date on Friday night.

Rameen's notational handiwork was passed along to a friend he'd met at Princeton. This was Joe, who was doing post-graduate work in Middle Eastern studies there after getting an undergraduate degree from Yale. Joe's specialty field was medieval espionage.

Princeton was then, as I understood it, a pretty good place to do such studies. It was one of those academic conduits for informal intergovernmental relations. When career professionals in the U.S. government know that one day they are going to be dealing with a currently unacceptable foreign power, some university starts importing 'academics' and 'scholars' from said foreign power to study and maybe do a little teaching on the side. These visitors lay the groundwork for all sorts of future political and economic exchanges when the political climate is finally right.

Yale played this role for China before more formal relations with the U.S. became feasible. One of Iran's top mullahs was teaching a course at Princeton when I was doing my own recruiting there.

But I digress.

Joe, my own new recruit, was a wunderkind of the Jewish variety. Which wasn't all that surprising since his great grandfather had been the Chief Rabbi of Bagdad. Joe had the kind of face you associate with Sinbad the Sailor, whose home base was Basra. He spoke six languages, attended raves in Tehran, and in terms of my proposed venture was a good catch because he was also a very fine pianist and composer. Joe was hot to get into this deal because he thought it would make him a fortune, not realizing until it was too late that the fact that I was organizing the deal made this very, very unlikely.

Rameen and Joe brought in Jonathan as our final Financial Harmonics partner. Jonathan was our instrument guy. More to the point, he had a home mixing studio where he could turn Joe's creations into playable recordings. Jonathan was then doing A&R for Polygram, and as far as I could figure, with that job at his age, he was lucky to stop screwing long enough to join our team.

I was now playing the middle aged father figure to a group that included an analytic maven who could convert stock movements into musical notation, a composer who added jazz riffs to this notation and riffed into the future, and an instrument meister who could record what came out the other side in a way that made it sound like high quality elevator music.

Our original business plan called for doing consulting work for technical analysts, the idea being that our output was a kind of a sound equivalent to their own traditional visually oriented technical analysis. Then maybe we'd produce CDs for financial professionals to play on their off hours.

It wasn't a bad business plan. But once the team was functioning and some sample recording actually made, I had pretty much lost interest in the project. I was making decent money. Why bother making a lot more? I had to work in a Wall Street milieu so as not go on welfare, but that didn't mean I had to adopt the values of the place.

Financial Harmonics ended up having just one gig. I had come across a newspaper story about a group of financial astrologers planning a get-together in Manhattan. I phoned the head of the group, told him we had a technique to musically compose the markets, asked if his members would like to see a demonstration.

"The music of the spheres!" he exclaimed.

"Absolutely," I agreed. "As above, so below."

My long ago ex-wife Suzanne had been into astrology so I remembered phrases like "as above, so below" that I'd been obliged to master while we were together. Once upon a time I'd even run a small and amazingly unprofitable company called Captain Astro's Out-Front T-Shirts. It manufactured tops with an individual's own zodiacal chart emblazoned on its front, which did away with the need to speak with a person you'd just met. All you had to do was check out his or her imprinted birth chart to know their entire personality. I believe this venture sold a total of five T-shirts.

"You'll make a great addition to our meeting," said the financial astrologers' program chairman.

There was one hurdle to clear before we could actually do our number there. I had to tell the guy who ran my department at Bloomberg that I and another member of his staff were taking part in this astrologers' program.

I explained the situation in a direct and forthright manner. As he listened I surmised that his early view that he'd hired a very smart and efficient employee was now tempered by the suspicion that this person (me) might actually be a wingnut.

When I finished explaining he was silent for a moment. Then looking me straight in the eye he said with considerable feelings: "Please, just don't let them know you work for us."

"Sure, Bill. No problemo," I replied.

The financial astrologers gathering in a midtown Manhattan hotel drew a pretty good crowd. Most were women who looked like aging relics of a then fast-fading New Age consciousness revolution, a remnant of which had generous divorce settlements that left them with the wherewithal to seek investment guidance from the heavens.

Our competition for attention that day was ludicrously weak. It consisted of two middle aged, male, professional astrologers trolling for clients with horoscopes for companies whose stocks, they claimed, were sure to rise in coming months because the companies' moons were in Virgo and their Venus on the cusp of Pluto. Or maybe Plato. Both these horoscope casters had enough hair growing out of their ears to weave a carpet, and oozed the kind of desperation for clients you see among gamblers in Atlantic City who were down to their last chip.

When it was our turn I rose from my chair and looked back at my three young and fresh-faced associates, feeling very like a Financial Harmonics Fagan about to send his Oliver Twists off to pick the pockets of distracted swells. I made a few opening comments that suggested I knew a little something about the relation of what goes on above and how that is related below here on earth. I then worked in the idea that our music-of-the-spheres was really just an advanced form of traditional technical analysis. After which I introduced Joe, who proceeded to blow away the audience with a virtuoso performance of "IBM 1994."

By the time Joe finished I probably could have sold half the audience shares in the Holland Tunnel. I certainly could have sold them shares in Financial Harmonics. Or signed up a goodly number of them to receive high-priced predictions on whatever stock Joe composed in the future. Or any stocks we happened to like for other reasons.

But hey, why bother? By this time Joe, Rameen, Jonathan and I all had better things to do with our lives than play out this exotic con. Rameen was about to quit Bloomberg and go off to Rio to share an apartment on Copa Cabana Beach with an old college pal. Joe had started his own gold trading company in Dubai. Jonathan was considering a return to law school.

Financial Harmonics was always more of a conceptual art project than a full-fledged gorilla raid in any case. A short story that was temporarily brought to life to show the relationship between fantasy and stock market predictions. Once this had been shown, it was time to move on to other things.

So why did these 'other things' lead to writing satirical poetry? Like most everything else in my life it was the product of a stumble here, a stumble there, and there I was.

I have a prose background when it comes to financial satire. In the 1980s I did a financial advice column with satirical trimmings for the Boston Phoenix; did a series of straight financial satire columns for the Los Angeles Times; and had pieces in this vein that ran in places like The Wall Street Journal, the Atlanta Constitution, and the Chicago Tribune. Some of this work was compiled into a little book titled *Planet Of The Financial Planners*, which helped land me my Bloomberg job.

It was fun work. Mocking one's financial betters in high profile media is always a source of joy. But I also often found the response to some of this prose satire depressing.

Consider what happened with two of what I thought were light-hearted satires that ran in the Wall Street Journal. One was a suggestion that we turn the Internal Revenue Service's tax collecting functions over to private firms that would really come down on tax deadbeats. I noted in this piece that such private revenuers were called publicans in biblical times, and were usually classed with lepers on the era's social scale. I noted as well that private tax collectors were a primary cause of the French Revolution according to Alexis DeToqueville.

You wouldn't think that with qualifiers such as these the piece could possibly fail to be recognized as satire. After it appeared in the Journal, I nevertheless got a call from someone on a Republican senator's staff wanting to get together to discuss how my idea could be turned into policy.

In another Journal piece I suggested that children should be given instruction in financial planning starting in kindergarten. You know. So the little ones could begin getting prepped for the rat race at five or six. Shortly after this appeared I heard that they were working to develop such a teaching program at the University of Iowa

I thus came to understand the problem writing satirical prose on financial subjects. Life was outrunning imagination here at every turn. Besides, there were already too many other people writing financial satire in prose. Some were doing it really, really well. Why enter a field with so many talented competitors?

Generally speaking, there are two ways to rise to the top of a profession. One is to study diligently, work long and hard, stick with it for decades. The other way is to invent the profession— or at least become one of its very few serious practitioners. I am almost always drawn to the latter approach. So I was naturally drawn to satirizing the financial world in verse.

Some great poets have functioned for a time in the world of business, finance, and related professions. James Joyce (banking) and Wallace Stevens (insurance) immediately come to mind. It's also true that a fair number of poems by other famous poets past dealt directly or indirectly with investing and markets—usually with disdain or outright loathing.

It occurred to me, however, that our own times were especially needful of poetry that covers this ground on a regular, appropriately disrespectful basis. We not only live in a world more dominated by markets than at any other time in human history, markets have attracted some of the world's best minds. Minds that in previous centuries were drawn to scholasticism,

talmudism, and the intricacies of predestination theory, were
in our own time focused on concocting exotic new financial
instruments whose most obvious virtue was that they generated
great wealth for their creators and these creators' employers
while doing little or nothing for everybody else.

Were there a great many perfect targets here for satirical verse?
Sure. But there were other reasons to write financial verse as
well. It didn't only have to skewer. Nor even just entertain. I
thought it could actually educate.

Poetry can render complicated thoughts into condensed forms. If
it rhymes, this verse also becomes much easier to memorize.

These simple insights got me into writing a running commentary
of financial markets in rhyme. The work gradually expanded to
include political subjects with financial connections (how, after
all, can you separate politics from markets in America today).
From there it progressed into a gorilla campaign.

 got the inspiration for my first financial poem when I stumbled
on one written by Ogden Nash in an old issue of The New
Yorker. His poem was a clever commentary on the high price
of real estate in Manhattan. Along with the social satire element
of the work, what I found inspirational here was that Nash used
the verse structure of a famous poem by Christopher Marlowe to
make his point in rhyme. Marlowe's "The Passionate Shepherd
To His Love."

Hey, I thought. If Ogden Nash could knock off poor dead
old Chris Marlowe to produce a commentary on the price of

Manhattan real estate in the 1930s, why couldn't I use the same verse structure to make a point about the contemporary stock market? Hence, my first financial verse, "The Passionate Broker To His Client." It went like this:

The Passionate Broker To His Client

Invest with me and be my client,
And we will all the markets troll,
For bargains and appealing yields,
In local stocks and foreign fields.

And we will take the long-term view,
Winning a bunch and losing a few,
Heeding the Fed and Abby Cohen,
Knowing we need never go it alone.

And I will balance all they holdings,
And never burden thee with scoldings,
I'll wear the dunce cap for thy failings
Accepting blame for thy derailings.

A condo large and mortgage free
You'll buy while on an earnings spree,
A closet full of minks and ermines,
A car designed by Swedes or Germans.

No more those nasty calls you'll get,
Demanding payment for old debt,
And if these goodies make thee pliant,
Come trade with me and be my client.

Our research staff shall hunt and find,
The treasures that will blow thy mind,
If these enrichers thy heart make pliant,
Then trade with me and be my client.

Glomming another poet's verse structure and toying with the original's meaning is old hat. This particular poem by Marlowe, in fact, has had countless reinventions, the most famous of which is probably Sir Walter Raleigh's "The Nymph's Reply To The Shepherd" penned shortly after Marlowe's own shepherd creation appeared.

Old hat to people who know poetry, however, came as a revelation to me. An inspiration, too, because I quickly discovered I not only had a peculiar gift for reworking great poets' rhyme structures and substituting new words for theirs, my knock-offs imparted a contemporary markets sensibility.

Once I got into doing this I found it hard to stop. I penned a tribute (of sorts) to heroic Wall Street felons keying off Henley's "Invictus" that I titled "Convictus." Since grade school I had been tormented by an inability to rid my mind of Kilmer's atrocious paean to the arboreal world, "Trees," until I did a version titled "Ts," a poem about Treasury bills that finally freed me. The last lines of Kilmer's original ran: "Poems are made by fools like me/But only God can make a tree." My own closer read: "Junk abounds that's triple-Cs/But only Sam can issue Ts."

My production seemed to swell week by week. Soon Shakespeare's "Shall I Compare Thee" in my fevered brain came out "Shall I Declare Thee," a putative tax evader's quandary; Richard Lovelace's "To Jucasta, Going To The Wars" found its market incarnation in my "Honey, I'm Off To The Futures Pits;" With a mall developer in mind, Samuel Taylor Coleridge's "Kubla Khan" was reborn as "Irwin Kahn;" Abby Cohen was much in the news then so I retooled Lord Byron's "She Walks In Beauty Like The Night" into "She Walks To Work At Goldman Sachs;"

On and on it went. Leigh Hunt's tender "Jenny Kiss'd Me" became a considerably less tender "Greenspan Stiff'd Me;"

Alfred Lord Tennyson saw heroic stupidity in "The Charge Of The Light Brigade," I saw just plain advertising-spawned stupidity in my "The Plight Of The Charge Brigade;" I reconfigured Henry Wadsworth Longfellow's "Excelsior" into "Alka-Seltzer."

This early phase was largely devoid of political commentary. After re-reading Emily Dickinson's "I Never Saw A Moor," however, how could I possibly miss the chance to turn it into "I Never Met Al Gore." My updated version of this classic opened with the lines: "I never met Al Gore/I never heard George Bush/ But still I know that one's a bore/And one just prattles mush."

When I began writing this light financial verse I thought I was in the perfect place to get it into print. I was working as a senior editor on Bloomberg's flagship publication, (then running under the name Bloomberg Magazine, later renamed Markets Magazine). Though this publication and the company generally focused on hard financial reportage and promotion of company products, there was also a recognition that Bloomberg's subscribers and readers liked to be entertained. There were thus also features about new boy toys, good places to eat, book reviews (I wrote some of these), and a not insignificant amount of other cultural coverage.

A company power play was wresting the magazine from the man who created it (and who had hired me) and putting it into the hands of new managers, These newcomers grandly announced that the magazine would have a major revamping, and they would welcome suggestions for anything that might set it apart from other magazines in this crowded field.

I figured my financial verse filled this bill perfectly. Sure, it was satirical, but it wasn't outright hostile to markets. Beyond that it oozed inside knowledge of actual market operations. Since I was already on the payroll, there wouldn't even be any extra costs adding it as a new feature.

Naturally, with all these things going for it, my suggestion for a regular financial verse column in the magazine was rejected. So what else was new?

This was the same kind of rejection I got when trying to convince book editors in the mid-1980s that I had a new way of viewing the environment-economic nexus. Back then it was "we love the environment, too, and know how important it is, unfortunately…" This time around it was "we love poetry, too, and know how important it is, unfortunately…"

Editors as a class are the most conservative people on the planet. They never really want anything new, they're just looking for new variants of old things, seeking to produce retreads of past successes. The super abundance of remainders that long plagued the publishing industry proved as much. The redundancy of articles one finds in journals in the same field today illustrates how this still plays out in the world of magazines.

Organizations like Bloomberg embodied this endless retread pattern perfectly. They employed very bright people to do endlessly repetitive versions of the same stories and features. Bloomberg wasn't a company that honored creative intelligence, which maybe is a good thing for people involved with financial services, because outfits that have truly honored creative intelligence haven't always ended well. Enron immediately comes to mind.

Clearly, Bloomberg was not my professional (or my gorilla) destiny. Just a way station to rest and save enough to gorilla on elsewhere. So about the same time as the company's founder, Mike Bloomberg, ran off to become mayor of New York, I quit to become a full-time financial poet.

Within six months of leaving I had my first book of financial poetry in print with a commercial publisher (*Songs Of Wall*

Street), and a regular financial poetry reading gig on The
Marketplace Morning Report broadcast on National Public
Radio. I was making other radio appearances on BBC and AP
Radio, and television appearances on FNN's Power Lunch.
Profiles of my financial verse ran in the New York Post,
Washington Post, and USA Today, and my poems were turning
up in literally dozens of other print and Internet media. My
wallstreetpoet.com website was attracting several thousand
visitors every week. Tidbits of my financial satire in rhyme were
even featured on the website of Poetry Magazine, this country's
most prestigious poetry publication.

It was great fun. It was also gratifying in a way I now considered
almost predictable. I had tried to convince people in positions of
power and authority (this time my employers at Bloomberg) that
financial verse was an obviously entertaining project that a lot of
people would find worthwhile. When these folks in positions of
power and authority couldn't see the obvious, I went on to prove
the idea myself.

Something important was nonetheless missing. Something an
easily contented chimp might let slide, but a gorilla couldn't
tolerate for long. I wasn't pissing off anyone.

Though my financial verse was often mildly mocking, it was
never really cruel or even especially biting. I don't dislike
markets or the people that pull their levers. Indeed, I find market
machinations intellectually fascinating and rife with all sorts of
unintended and amusing quirks. When it came to the big-time
market players themselves, except for their unseemly obsession
with money, I generally found them pretty good company.

So after awhile I began doing another kind of commentary
in rhyme that would allow a greater latitude for my too long
quiescent gorilla inclinations. Political poems. Or more
accurately, political commentary in rhyme. From my perspective
the beauty of this decision was not only that it was a more

challenging use of my talents, it would also illustrate some
present failings of both the American poetry establishment and
our media opinion-making establishment.

A bit about me and poetry. Not being involved with poetry
before I started writing some in my late fifties, I had no reason
to think about its role in people's lives. Once I did start thinking
about it, I very quickly realized how astonishingly minor this
role has become.

Astonishing when one considers how important poetry has
always been before in human affairs: As a means to articulate
our most profound thoughts; express our deepest religious
feelings; as a great entertainment, both by itself and in tandem
with music; as sexual foreplay second in importance only to
alcohol in terms of efficacy.

The role of poetry in politics has traditionally been equally
significant. The first true political talking heads were bards.
Before there was even writing, members of a ruling class never
really knew where they stood until the old blind guy with the
lyre posted the insiders' scorecard in rhyme.

Epic poems not only created the myths that defined the political
ideals of Europe's Middle Ages, they conferred legitimacy on
rulers of the period. Poets have done as much to bring many new
nations into existence as politicians or generals. On the world's
battlefields, countless men have died reciting a poem, and in
places like Japan, writing one as their personal farewell to the
world.

So where, I wondered, were America's own political poets in the first years of the new millennium that we were entering? And since many of the great political debates of our era are hashed out (and hacheted out) on this country's Op Ed and opinion pages, why weren't these pages filled with political poetry of the right and left?

This question popped into my head when I happened to come across a poem by Percy Shelley—"England in 1819." An angry and devastatingly incisive political critique, it's a poem of just 14 lines and less than 100 words that still brings into clear and vivid view the condition of post-Napoleonic England.

Here's a taste of how Shelley evoked the corruption of an entire political culture in just three lines and 25 words of this poem: "Rulers who neither see, nor feel, nor know,/But leech-like to their fainting country cling,/Till they drop, blind in blood, without a blow…"

Wow. Try to beat that in prose.

Shelley called poets the legislators of the world. But it seemed to me that he and poets like him really functioned more as Op Ed writers of the world, and that poetry of the kind they wrote had at least as much right to appear on today's Op Ed pages as the 750-word prose pieces that mostly fill these spaces.

Carrying this notion a bit further, Robert Frost once described poetry as "the best possible way of saying anything." Would it not be grand, I thought, if this best possible way of saying anything turned up regularly on Op Ed pages where public policies that affect us all are debated and shaped?

Since it had been so easy for me to rise into the top ranks of financial verse and appear with this work in so many high profile media, I figured it would be even easier to get my political verse

on Op Ed and opinion pages, and thereby help other poets get
their own political commentary there. Heck, financial verse
was a bauble, a novelty, while political verse had a long and
honorable history, something we really needed in these per'lous
times. Political battles were being fought that required every
form of creative weaponry employed to the fullest.

To help get this ball rolling I started writing some political verse,
posted scores of examples on my own wallstreetpoet.com site,
sent a big bunch to Op Ed editors of every major (and a lot of
minor) newspapers in the United States, as well as to all manner
of poetry publications. Beyond the verse itself, I also sent essays
about the importance of getting more political poetry before
much larger audiences to these same entities.

The result? Failure. Still, the experience was instructive. It
taught me a lot about both the worlds of American poetry and
the American opinion shaping media. Things I believe are worth
passing along which other gorilla poets might find useful in their
own future raids on these establishments.

If Ernie Kovacs wasn't the funniest man who ever lived, he was
certainly in the top two. I still wake up some nights laughing
about the antics of some of his creations like the Nairobi Trio,
three guys in gorilla suits (I'm a sucker for gorilla suits) making
music (of sorts), who brilliantly combined cerebral humor with
Larry, Moe and Curley slapstick.

An even funnier Kovacs comic invention was Percy
Dovetonsils. Dovetonsils was an excruciatingly precious fellow

who exhibited the ethereal mannerisms many people have in recent decades associated with this art form. Alas, though greatly exaggerated, Dovetonsils didn't totally miss the mark when it came to the kind of poetry he dribbled.

Today's official keepers of the poetry flame continue to encourage endlessly introspective, unstructured work that's geared to winning juried prizes and the approval of a tight little circle of learned professionals. To help ensure that only a deserving cognoscenti have access to it, they have largely assigned the most populist element of poetry, rhyme, to the establishment doggerel pile.

The result? Most Americans don't give a damn about poetry. Why should they? It doesn't give a damn about them. It doesn't speak to them about big issues important to them in ways they can easily follow much less remember.

Which brings us to the matter of political poetry. Yes, there was a flood of protest poetry over our involvement in Iraq. But why should anti-war poems be the totality of political verse commentary? Why not poems about tax laws, the state of our political parties, Supreme Court decisions, health care, income inequality, campaign finance reform, pay-to-play government contracting—all the gut issues that bring forth the institutional approaches that order our public lives—poetry that enriches the national debate, changes political views, provides better ways of understanding and altering contemporary political realities.

Missing, missing, all missing. Such poetry isn't being produced in sufficient quantity and quality to merit a place in the closely followed media perused by our political ruling class or a large chunk of the voting class—rap and poetry slam verse, with their more limited audiences, don't fill the void.

America's officially approved poets today just don't get this or just don't seem to care. They're holed up in private ruminations, satisfied with genteel obscurity played out in obscure journals. They've been captured and incarcerated by themselves and an establishment in prissy little hermit cells that pass in their own minds as exalted domains of high culture.

In consequence they fail miserably to carry out what has always been one of the most important missions of their craft—making poetry a potent force for positive political change.

Alright. The response I got from the poetry community regarding political verse was non-existent. Maybe that wasn't surprising. But you'd think that the people who control this country's Op Ed and opinion pages would be more receptive to the idea.

What I was suggesting, after all, was not a particular point of view that might get them in trouble with folks holding different views. I was simply suggesting that they make use of another means of political expression, one that got across notions from all sides of the political spectrum.

To me, one of the appeals of poetry to opinion-seeking readers is obvious. Any reasonably intelligent person who has reached middle age has read hundreds, and perhaps thousands, of prose opinion pieces—and can't remember the first or last lines of any of them. This same reasonably intelligent person having reached middle age and having received even a middling education can recite, verbatim, a fair amount of poetry. Especially the easy to memorize rhyming variety.

As for being a non-prose anomaly on opinion pages, that's really a non-issue. There are already political cartoons there. If you're already using this non-prose cartoon medium for political commentary, why not poetry, too?

Except for snippets of verse that appear when a new poet laureate is named, and perhaps a cutsie rhyme to herald the first day of spring, these spaces are poetry deserts. An ongoing flow of pertinent, punchy, powerful, memorable, and timely commentary in verse about nitty-gritty political realities of interest to the widest possible audience is almost nowhere to be found.

I banged my well scarred and bandaged gorilla head against this stone wall for a couple of years. Until there suddenly appeared what seemed like the perfect medium in the perfect place to reach the perfect audience for what I was trying to sell.

In 2004 the owners of the San Francisco Examiner decided to publish a new daily, the Washington Examiner. The pre-publicity for this new pub emphasized it planned to cover the Washington political scene in new ways and it was very receptive to new ideas about how to do so.

You'd think, having heard this "we're open to new and innovative approaches" so many times before from people who would then prove themselves never really interested in doing so, I wouldn't bother contacting the editors of this budding journal. But of course I did. And this time it looked like the effort would actually bear fruit.

An editor at the Examiner got back to me after checking my credentials saying yes, they would run my political commentaries in verse on a regular basis. My happiness at this response lasted all of 48 hours, when this same editor got back again and said his decision had been reversed because his bosses had decided no poetry on the editorial pages.

No reason was given. None was really needed. The poetry establishment had so perverted the notion that poetry could not and should not be a vehicle for political discourse, but had to be kept pure, just a medium for emoting deep personal feelings, that the editorial Masters of the Universe wanted nothing to do with these precious bozos. I assume that the editor who originally bought into my own proposal was appropriately disciplined for not understanding this.

There is a happy ending here, though. Not for me, but for the kind of satirical political verse I was writing.

In 2004 Calvin Trillin's book of satirical political verse was published and made the New York Times best-seller list. Though this work did not trigger a huge upsurge in opinion page use of political poetry, Trillin's best selling illustrations of what's possible with this medium, both as an entertainment vehicle and mode of criticism, provided me with the excuse to move on.

And what the heck, while doing so generally, I still putter a bit in this field. In recent years I have gotten my own regular column to spout political commentary in rhyme. I do the endpaper poems for every issue of The Progressive Populist. Here's five examples of my work in this genre:

1.

The Supreme Court has recognized a corporation's constitutional right to political expression. It even recognized a corporation's right to religious expression. So shouldn't the right of corporations to marry — not just other corporations via mergers but people — be recognized, too? And if a guy like me also happens to have a thing for Hewlett-Packard, shouldn't I have the right to pop the question?

Dear HP, Please Marry Me

Dear HP, please marry me
And soon enough we'll make them see
That man and firm can find a way
To mate, the heck what skeptics say.

Our courtship past was long and bumpy
On the road to rumpy pumpy
But soon, I'm sure, we'll be much freer
Thanks to Antonin Scalia.

His law proclaims we're both the same
So will you deign to share my name
And stride the world, head high, a queen
As Helett-Packard Silverstein.

2.

Were William Shakespeare here today and facing an April 15
deadline to file his income taxes, he might well be inspired to
write a sonnet very like this one.

Shall I Declare Thee

Shall I declare thee to the IRS
Thou cap gain piddling and so well hidden?
If I get caught it means a real mess
And audits on other deals I've ridden.
Sometimes it's best a small gain to ignore
When reaching for it brings unwanted heat
Far bigger gains then exit profit's door
As agents come, thy assets to delete.

But still a gain's a thing not easy lost,
And passing up a credit smacks of sin.
Each small increase to revenuers tossed
Could better go to charity or kin.
So this I'd rather do, risk a pickle
Than give those leeches one extra nickel.

3.

A Monarchy Of Money

In days of yore the rich would seek a needy candidate,
And legally (though quietly) his campaign chest inflate.
Both giver and receiver liked the tradeoff here just fine,
One got himself more access, one could buy more TV time.

But these days folks with money have devised a better plan;
It's a lot more cost effective, it shuts out the middleman.
Instead of buying influence with others they select,
They run themselves for office and buy public posts direct.

The process here is simple, it comes down to TV buys;
When you spend big on this medium, your numbers always rise.
Perfect family, hard hat workers, ethnic types, a waving flag,
Are the content of your message, which gets shown till viewers gag.

While talking heads may hold their nose at such crude repetition,
It's the perfect way (just ask the pros) to beat the competition.
In mayors' contests coast to coast, in House and Senate races,
Rich nobodies who buy the tube end up with smiling faces.

So a monied power seeker need no longer use a beard,
He can buy an office outright and no one now thinks it's weird.
Though perhaps some free speech theorists see here a prospect sunny,
Wiser heads fear ever greater strides toward a monarchy of money.

4.

A water carrier for the British army in India was the hero of
Kipling's poem, "Gunga Din." Fed Chairman Ben Bernanke
became the great carrier of water for Wall Streeters after the
2008 market crash. My Kipling-esque Gunga Din knockoff—
Gunga Ben.

Gunga Ben

You may praise free market's power
With stocks in endless flower
And home prices looking like they'll never top;
But comes the sound of crashing
There's just one place you'll be looking
And a'begging for the horrid drop to stop.

Sure you spend your working time
In that well-paid Wall Street clime
Claimin' you're a master of the universe;
And the crew you bring together
Swears you need no outside fetter
'Til your arrogance brings down that crashing curse.

Then its "Ben! Ben! Ben!
We need a huge Fed handout once again;"
Though all others he's ignorin'
For you guys Ben is adorin'
Always saving The Street's bacon, Gunga Ben.

5.

Almost all the very worst ideas now crapping up American
politics originate or are tarted up in conservative think tanks.
Here's an insider's description of who does the tarting and how
it's done.

Michael Silverstein

Confessions Of A Think Tanker

For many long years I felt ineffectual
A misunderstood and ignored intellectual
My theories (though brilliant) were hooted and hissed
By colleagues and others their value dismissed.
But still I did labor to make them more statable
In hopes that one day they'd become more debatable
And those that opposed them for reasons nefarious
Would meet a just fate that was most deleterious.

In the tank, in the tank, in my Beltway think tank,
Part campus,
Part book barn,
Part nut house,
Part bank.

It's true a great thinker on great ideas thrives
But it's also quite true that we have private lives
To best change perceptions and settle old scores
We need the support of big buck sinecures.
The best thinking's done on a surfeit of calories
And tends to improve in tandem with salaries
This linkage ain't found in a staid university
Not to mention such places' diverting diversity.

In the tank, in the tank, in my Beltway think tank,
Part campus,
Part book barn,
Part nut house,
Part bank.

It was only by chance that I found my true nesting
The place in my heart I had always been questing
I'd published a screed, arcane and voluminous

So riddled with bile, some tagged it bituminous.
It seemed for a time to attract no attention
Except the occasional snide condescension
Until came that call from a hunter of heads
Who asked if I'd ever considered Op Eds.

In the tank, in the tank, in my Beltway think tank,
Part campus,
Part book barn,
Part nut house,
Part bank.

I'd always deemed Op Eds a medium trivial
So compact one's points couldn't be unequivial
Yet write one I did, laced with fury and gumption
Too high-brow (I figured) for pop press consumption.
But turn up it did, on a blatt's viewpoints page
Where it went on to garner both pro and con rage
My head hunter pitched it to tanks with fat coffers
And got back a slew of paid thinker job offers.

In the tank, in the tank, in my Beltway think tank,
Part campus,
Part book barn,
Part nut house,
Part bank.

I now have a slot as cushy as jello
I'm called a researcher and visiting fellow
I analyze trends, write books in a gush
All published before being pulped into slush
On TV they love me on talking head junction
A chicken and peas night is my fav'rite function
At fund-raising meets, rich egos I lather
With partisan factoids and scholarly blather.

In the tank, in the tank, in my Beltway think tank,
Part campus,
Part book barn,
Part nut house,
Part bank.

I longed for a place where they pay by the syllable
Where spewing odd visions and ideas is billable
Where the kinkiest, crankiest, odd scheme devisors
Can train to become presidential advisors.
A shadowy power most people don't see
Is now wielded by thinkers-for-hire like me
My nostrums are slick, and my come backs are rapid
Just perfect for pols whose own brains have gone vapid.

In the tank, in the tank, in my Beltway think tank,
Part campus,
Part book barn,
Part nut house,
Part bank.

Aside from writing political commentary in verse for the
Progressive Populist, I've pretty much moved on from my
gorilla poetry phase. Though there have been a few brief lapses.
One involved the Federal Reserve.

Poets in residence have become a commonplace these days.
Every college seems to have one, every community. These
"residencies," which rarely if ever actually come with a living

space, have evolved into a way to honor some time server in the English department without actually raising this person's salary, and at the community level, as a way to keep a local eccentric happy enough not to interrupt city council meetings with rants about the need to improve local services.

So what institution needs an image makeover more than any other, I asked myself? Which one has so flagrantly served the interests of financial markets more than any other, financial markets that have been subjects of so much of my own verse? Which institution could benefit the most by seeming to appear culturally sensitive? And since I now live in Philly, which one could offer me a poet-in-residence gig without me having to travel out of town for the required monthly readings?

Ask questions like these and the answer is obvious. The Federal Reserve Bank right in my present hometown.

I emailed everyone listed on the Philadelphia Federal Reserve Bank website and got not a single reply. It was almost as if they thought this was some kind of joke. Or maybe even that I was making fun them.

When this poet-in-residence idea flopped, I took one more shot at benefitting significantly from my financial verse. This one was not aimed at reaching out to an institution, but to a very rich person with a cultural bent and a desire for slavish praise. Here's the message I sent to those in this category I could contact by email:

Think You Have It All? You Don't! Not Without Having A Personal Poet On Retainer.

Sure you made a billion. Made it with a social media triumph that allows hordes of vacuous people to spend their days sharing pictures of their cats with millions of friends online. Or maybe with a brilliant derivative that destroyed the economic future of a small country in Europe.

You earned your billions. And you bought all the boy toys that were supposed to make you happy. You've even begun the laundering process of this money by giving bits of it to environmental and cultural organizations, thereby earning the right to be endlessly surrounded by chirping Gaian groupies and anorexic graduates with fine arts degrees and meaningless titles at large museums, all seeking to glom even more from your bottomless pile.

But it's not enough. Why? Because every Tom, Dick and Jane billionaire is doing the same — except Jane who bought a lot of girlie goodies instead of boy toys.

So now you're thinking: Mike, how do I set myself apart from the billionaire herd? Here's my answer: With a personal poet on retainer. Someone to elevate just another multi-million dollar wedding, christening or bas mitzvah into an event that will ring down the ages. And not only bring you this singular joy to which only great wealth is entitled, but memorable rhyming discomfort to your enemies as well. For the poet's quill can sting like an arrow as well as happily tenderize like a good stool softener.

Interested? You betcha. But you'd best get in touch with me promptly. Before someone who hates you and has even more money gets to me first.

Serious inquiries only

There were no serious inquiries. Oh, well.

VIII.
More To Do, Always
(A Gorilla Sums Up His Past, Looks To The Future)

What were the lessons learned before I went a-gorillaing that contributed to my thinking and actions on later gorilla battlefields? What had I learned from a wrist chomping Yetta, a Yiddish speaking Irish bagel baker's son, a military career inaugurated with half a cup of borrowed piss, a violence prone rabbi, a laundry drop off at a former German concentration camp, living in a windmill, cleaning a royal palace, and being a photographic stand-in for a movie star?

I learned that few things are too silly in this world not to be commonplace. That you get by with a little unexpected help from strangers. That if you keep moving you often find yourself in interesting places and situations. That religion and politics can be very good things when kept separate but become toxic and poisonous when mixed. That a good photographer and the right lighting can make almost anyone look good. And that in human affairs dumb luck almost always trumps everything else.

From TV watching and reading in my pre-gorillaing days I also learned things of great worth. The most valuable lesson from the tube came from the *Doctor Who* series, and one of that series' chief villains, the Daleks.

Daleks looked like inverted trash cans with blister candy
skin and weapons resembling extended toilet plungers. They
nonetheless styled themselves "masters of the universe" and
used the memorable threat line, "resistance is futile." I always
remembered those looks and words when encountering people
in later years who fancied themselves masters of the universe
and believed opposition to themselves was always destined
to be futile. Such people sometimes turned out wrong on both
accounts.

A major literary inspiration came from reading Edmond
Rostand's play, *Cyrano de Bergerac*. One line in that play, "a
man does not fight to win," has always struck me as the essence
of behavioral wisdom.

Of course it's nice to win. But what's really important is fighting
honorably for what you think is right. Because in a fight against
a very strongly entrenched group or idea you're almost never
going to win.

So what. Just mutter a bit, feel sorry for yourself for awhile, then
go on and pick another good fight.

Looking ahead.

Life is so wonderfully imperfect. The ability of people to
make things far worse than they need to be, cleaving to ideas
hopelessly outmoded or just plain stupid, is endless. This is
thus a world created for gorillas. Year by year, month by month,
day by day, opportunities, nay, necessities for gorilla raids
proliferate.

I'm in my seventies now. Too old to get those ratty gorilla slippers out of the closet. But also far more skilled at the gorilla game generally, and better able to use a bigger chest of gorilla weapons. Sometime soon I'll go raiding again when something comes along that catches my fancy.

Little sparks, even if they fail to ignite great fires, always shine some light and provide a bit of warmth. And taking a whack or two at The Great Them is always great fun.

Winning is nice. Trying honorably and fulsomely without caring about winning or loosing is better.

Once more into the breach, dear friends. Once more.

Other books by Michael Silverstein:

The Devil's Dictionary Of Wall Street
Silverstein's Devil's Dictionary Of Wall Street takes an Ambrose
Bierce approach to today's overblown markets and their puffed up
denizens.

*The Chronicles Of Selig Cartwright, Goldman Sachs Washroom
Attendant*
An Everyman talks markets with a Wall Streetman in a place where
pretensions of superiority of any kind are impossible to retain for long.

A Dyspeptic's Guide To Contemporary American Politics (In Verse)
This collection offers up a hundred-and-one poems disdaining and
dissecting our presently dysfunctional politics—taking no prisoners
along the way.

Fifteen Feet Beneath Manhattan
A wild riff about very strange doings under the streets of Gotham.
Where all that stands in the way of New York City descending into
utter chaos is a bumbling reporter and a pistol-toting feminist with
anger issues.

The Bellman's Revenge
A very unusual private detective confronts a demented scientist and a
crazed Indian shaman, both seeking vengeance in a way that taps into
the secret fear of every traveler.

Murder At Bernstein's
The billionaire creator of a financial news empire wants to be elected
Mayor of Philadelphia. He looks like a shoe-in until the man who runs
his stock market music department is murdered.

www.ingramcontent.com/pod-product-compliance
Lightning Source LLC
Chambersburg PA
CBHW072005090426
42740CB00011B/2099